Shostakovich
His Life and Music

Shostakovich
His Life and Music

Brian Morton

HAUS
BOOKS
London

Originally published in
Great Britain in 2006 by
Haus Publishing Limited
26 Cadogan Court
London SW3 3BX

copyright © Brian Morton 2006

The moral right of the author has been asserted

A CIP catalogue record for this book
is available from the British Library

ISBN 1904950507
ISBN 9781904950509

Designed in Adobe InDesign CS2
and typeset in Adobe Garamond Premier Pro by
Rick Fawcett

Cover image courtesy of akg Images, London

Printed and bound by Graphicom, Vicenza, Italy

www.hauspublishing.co.uk

Contents

Introduction

Introduction

Two photographs, taken some dozen years apart. Both show a squat, bespectacled man who one immediately and instinctively characterises – even without knowing his name – as guarded and intense. In both images, he is far from home. Were not the occasions respectively peaceful and celebratory, one might suspect he was a prisoner. In a very real sense, he was.

In the later photograph, one might say that he is at least among friends and fellow-artists; fellow-socialists, too, if the public persona and role are to be believed. It was taken in the George Hotel, Edinburgh, in August 1962, during the city's renowned annual arts festival. The men flanking him might as well be warders for all the warmth in his expression, though perhaps the lack of a common language made for a certain awkwardness. The two men are, respectively, a poet and a fellow-composer. Hugh MacDiarmid is a literary maverick, marked by deep apparent contradictions. His public name is also a mask, a pseudonym for Christopher Grieve; his politics have always seemed muddled, a mixture of Communist internationalism, intense Scottish nationalism, with an admixture of Major Douglas's quasi-fascist Social Credit thrown in.

The other man is Ronald Stevenson, an adopted Scot born in the north of England – the musicologist Nicholas Slonimsky described him as "Brythonic" – who has spent some time in South Africa, an experience that has further sharpened his instinct for political justice. He has come to present their honoured guest with the score of a huge piano work, some say the longest single movement piece ever written for the instrument. In much the way classical composers created tributes to a revered ancestor by using the letters B-A-C-H as a musical cell (in German notation that is sounded B flat-A-C-B natural), Stevenson's piece is called *Passacaglia for DSCH*.

The earlier photograph was taken in March 1949 in the even more sumptuous surroundings of the Waldorf-Astoria Hotel in New York City. At the extreme left (no pun intended) is A A Fadayev, secretary-general of the Union of Soviet Writers. Opposite him, in profile, is the British science fiction writer Olaf Stapledon, over whom towers the smiling Arthur Miller, already a celebrated playwright. Next to Fadayev, light-suited and holding a cigarette, is the 26 year old Norman Mailer whose shy, averted gaze sits oddly with the arrogant smirk

that plays across his lower features. Lionised though he might have been since the publication of his best-selling war novel *The Naked and the Dead*, self-possessed though he undoubtedly was by temperament, he must have felt slightly overwhelmed to find himself standing alongside one of the hero-artists of the late war, the composer of a symphony that in 1942 had been broadcast to millions worldwide in the most difficult circumstances imaginable and which had become the musical symbol of wartime resistance to Nazism. Fifteen years earlier, an American concert-goers association had voted Sibelius's Symphony No 2 the greatest musical work of all time. By 1949, with Sibelius already some years into the long silence that marked his final three decades, no one would have questioned that the greatest living symphonist – and a master in other forms as well – was Dmitri Dmitrievich Shostakovich.

Dmitri Shostakovich photograped on a visit to Frankfurt in 1948

Photographed at the Cultural and Scientific Conference for World Peace at the Waldorf-Astoria Hotel in New York. Shostakovich sits in he front row with S A Gerasimov, Olaf Stapledon, Alex Fadayev and Dr R E G Armattoe.

Mailer's air of faint discomfort may have been exacerbated by the knowledge that he was just about to launch a savage and uncompromising attack on the man who had despatched Fadayev and Shostakovitch as Soviet representatives to a cultural and scientific conference on world peace organised by the National Council of the Arts, Sciences and Professions. Mailer astonished not just the other guests but his wife and close friends in the audience by taking a strong anti-Stalinist line indeed, Trotskyite line suggesting with impressive prescience that not just the United States but also the Soviet Union was drifting towards state capitalism. "I have come here as a Trojan horse", he declared. That ironically, was the view taken by the American authorities to the whole event.The US State Department had already denounced the conference as

ДМИТРИЙ ДМИТРИЕВИЧ ШОСТАКОВИЧ

a Communist front, a view which echoed – or orchestrated – the anti-Communist protest and picket outside the Waldorf-Astoria on the night of the conference's gala dinner.

The guest speakers on that occasion were Dr Harlow Shapley of Harvard University and Shostakovich. The Perroquet Room was an entirely appropriate location for the composer's address, which had him parrot the standard Soviet line on the duty of artists to promote a realistic and optimistic view of national life – "When abroad I feel myself to be a representative of the great Soviet people and of the world cultural centre– Moscow" – and to resist the abstract formalism and blandly tragic cosmopolitanism of bourgeois art. As reported in the *New York Times*, Shostakovitch said; "Here I must stress that Party criticism of formalism in Soviet music is a life-giving source of musical creativeness. It helps all of us to paralyse alien influences and completely devote our art to the people and the motherland". Shostakovitch had many times put his name and signature to words written for him by others. At least on this occasion he was not required to speak them aloud. The address was read by an interpreter. Whether he meant it, or the condemnation of Igor Stravinsky that followed, is a question that goes to the heart of what is seen as the Shostakovich enigma.

The wider context of his visit to America is revealing. A matter of weeks before he flew to America, Shostakovich had been a non-person, his work condemned and proscribed by Stalin's cultural commissar Andrei Zhdanov. It's one measure of the black ironies and perversities of life under the Soviet regime that when Zhdanov died in August 1948, six months after the *Glavrepertkom* (State Commission for Repetoire) edict that effectively denied Shostakovitch a living and free expression, Shostakovitch should have been quoted in an obituary article, praising "dear Andrei Alexandrovich" as a "man of wide education and extraordinary erudition", whose death was a "grievous, bitter loss".

Six months after that, Shostakovich received a late night telephone call from Joseph Stalin himself. Shostakovich had spent many a sleepless night over the previous decade and a half waiting for the midnight knock on the door that would signal his arrest and disappearance into the hungry maw of what became known as the GULAG; either that, or it represented the sharp pre-echo of the pistol shot that would end his life in some darkened cellar room. The life of Vsevolod Meyerhold, Shostakovich's dramatic mentor and one-time employer, had ended this way in the pre-war purges. In the event, Stalin merely "asked" him to attend the Cultural and Scientific Conference and, seemingly surprised that Shostakovich's work was still banned, lifted the proscription.

Such haphazard perversity is very much part of our received image of Soviet Communism, but American official attitudes and public opinion were every bit as fickle, even if the *volte-face* wasn't quite so rapid. On March 24th Shostakovich landed at New York's LaGuardia airport, where he was met by Mailer and by America's most distinguished composer Aaron Copland. The broadcast premiere of Shostakovitch's Seventh Symphony from Radio City had made him an international hero. The day after the première July 20 1942, he had appeared on the cover of *Time* magazine, wearing the helmet of a volunteer fireman. Seven years later, in a much-changed political climate – and possibly with the disillusionment of seeing a hero in the under-nourished, unfashionably dressed flesh – the response was decidedly lukewarm. Far from heroic, Shostakovich seemed shabby, neurasthenic, eternally hidden behind the spectacles he fiddled with constantly. In an issue published on the day the Soviet delegation flew home, *Time* magazine rounded on him sharply and other commentators noted with disgust how Shostakovich had apparently endorsed *Pravda*'s condemnation of fellow-composers and compatriots, Stravinsky and Prokofiev among them, as "decadents" and "lackeys" of the West.

If America had chilled to Shostakovich, he failed to warm to Americans. Recalling the visit, he railed at the triviality of American journalism and the excessively personal questions asked by American journalists. The wartime alliance had given way to a vast gulf of incomprehension, but had in any case been forged in spite of huge political and cultural differences. In a year haunted by "alien" sightings and UFO landings in an America that had resisted terrestrial invasion, there could have been no more otherworldly a visitor than Dmitri Shostakovich.

Americans of the time could only have had the dimmest understanding of how Shostakovich and his fellow-artists had lived, not just during a war which cost some 20,000,000 Russian lives but under a regime that since 1917 had practised terror on its own citizens. Fellow-travelling visitors from the US had included journalist John Reed, author of a highly sanguine account of the Bolshevik Revolution *Ten Days That Shook The World*, and given a hero's burial in the Kremlin Wall when he died of typhus in 1920, and Lincoln Steffens, who had gone to observe the Communist experiment and provided a highly serviceable and adaptable quote when he reported back "I have seen the future, and it works". Though there were steady rumblings of anxiety, not least among Mailer's new Trotskyite friends and the staff of the Trotskyite *Partisan Review*, originally published under the auspices of the John Reed Clubs, it wasn't until the revelations of the 20th Congress of the Soviet Communist Party in 1956 and Nikita Khrushchev's "secret" revelation of Stalin's "cult of the personality" that the true horrors of the Stalinist terror became widely known in the West. For the moment, Shostakovich was the – apparently willing – mouthpiece of an enemy state and of a political system violently inimical to the American way.

But how willing? What went on "behind those frightened, very intelligent eyes", as someone who met him rather later put it? Why were they frightened? And how did that formidable intelligence work under a regime where intelligence itself, let alone a critical intelligence, was feared and suppressed? Americans are popularly supposed to lack a sense of irony. For Russians of Shostakovitch's generation, irony was a genetic inheritance; and not just simple irony, but layers of it, like an onion.

At the final session of the Waldorf-Astoria conference, late in the evening, Shostakovich had sat down alone at the piano and played the second movement from his Symphony No 5 to the assembled delegates. This was the work which had been published 12 years earlier bearing the apparently self-denying recantation "A Soviet artist's response to just criticism". In the story of Dmitri Shostakovich, much is appearance. Getting at the reality underneath – or at least to some solid ground from which to make an objective judgement – is much harder. As we'll see in Chapter Four, it is difficult to tell whether the composer's "apology" was sincere, enforced, a merely routine obeisance, a terrified reaction to a climate of terror, or simply part of the complex anthropology of Russian life under the Soviet when opposition had be expressed in coded forms and where abjection might sarcastically suggest its opposite; these are long-standing, to some degree unanswerable, and to a further degree irrelevant questions.

Little remarked, compared to the premieres of the Fifth Symphony and later the Seventh, that cameo performance offers important symbolic pointers to what might be called "the Shostakovich problem". Here was a man far from home, sitting in the heart of the enemy's camp, in front of a polite audience but with hostile demonstrators outside, playing a nakedly stripped down version of one of his most famous and complex works, and the Scherzo movement at that. Shostakovich was all too aware how black the joke – which is what Scherzo means – actually was, and how painfully forced his expression. Much later, he said "Look at the way I'm smiling in the photographs. That was the smile of a condemned man. I answered all the idiotic questions in a daze and thought, When I get back it's over for me". It wasn't though. Shostakovich outlived his and his country's tormentor by more than two decades. The familiar caprices of state terror this time worked to spare him, though probably what protected Shostakovitch most was the very success, both at home and abroad, of the Fifth and Seventh Symphonies. By 1949, even though still profoundly suspect and required to suppress all personal elements in his work, he was too important and too prominent to be disappeared.

Right across the range of Shostakovich studies, from perspectives of the left and of the right, critics and biographers have found themselves hamstrung by the question of Shostakovitch's exact political sympathies – loyal Communist, visceral anti-Communist, loyal Communist disillusioned by Stalinism – and about the sincerity of his personal and asethetic opinions. Even an admiring bystander like rock musician Elvis Costello, a self-professed amateur student of Shostakovitch's work, expressed himself disappointed that Shostakovitch recently should have been "so rubbery of will" and a "stooge" of the state. It is one of this essay's modest contentions that Shostakovitch's apparent about-faces – and all is appearance in this story – camouflage a basic consistency of attitude and can only be understood, beat for beat, in the rapidly changing contexts of Soviet politics and cultural "policy". Somewhat more aggressively, it will also suggest that Shostakovich's admittedly strange career is not *sui generis*, not just in comparison to his Russian contemporaries but to the careers of many other great artists. What of Beethoven's disillusioned re-dedication of the "Eroica"

Symphony? The comparison is tricky, but not absurd. Does it not suggest a change of heart, or at least the necessity of responding to political contingency? In a similar way, why, when dealing with the vexed, but now largely resolved question of Shostakovitch's autobiographical *Testimony* (to which we'll come shortly), do the same critics never mention Robert Craft's remarkable – some would say incredible – recall of Stravinsky's conversations and comments? Do we distrust *Memories and Commentaries* and *Expositions and Developments* and reject Craft as a self-serving ventriloquist the way we have distrusted *Testimony* and condemned its "editor" Solomon Volkov as a forger?

It is from Craft, Stravinsky's friend and amanuensis (some would say ghost writer) that we have that vivid description of Shostakovitch's frightened eyes. Craft had the opportunity to observe him at close quarters during Stravinsky's much-feted, all-is-forgiven visit to Russia in 1962. Forgiven by the authorities, that is; Stravinsky himself was disinclined to forget past slights and calumny, and by Shostakovitch's own account offered one Party *apparatchik* the head of his walking stick to shake instead of his hand. What his account fails to mention is that a dozen years earlier, Shostakovitch himself had passively endorsed the Soviet condemnation of Stravinsky, despite his deep personal admiration of his fellow-composer's work. It's clear, from *Testimony* and elsewhere, that words had been put into his mouth. Though he distrusted Stravinsky's cosmopolitanism and may have envied not so much his international reputation – Shostakovitch was himself known throughout the West – but the seeming *ease* of it. Where Shostakovitch was admired for his courage, toughness, the mixture of tragedy and satire in his work, Stravinsky was feted as a superstar, a man equally at ease in Paris, New York or Los Angeles.

The two composers met twice in early October 1962. They flanked their hostess at a formal reception and were thrown together again a few days later at the banquet that marked the climax of Stravinsky's visit. It was here that Craft observed Shostakovitch, handsomer than expected and almost "boyish-looking", but nervously gnawing at his fingers, chain smoking, and looking poised (if that's the right word) between uncertainty and tears. At least in 1962, the composer could not have feared death on his return home, but the shadow of Stalin – dead almost ten years – and of "Stalinism" was no lighter and no less extensive. There had been, however, a major shift in Soviet cultural policy, not least in attitude to "problematic" artists like Shostakovich. He may have felt galled that a figure like Stravinsky could make a reputation and a significant fortune abroad – he was, after all, the first classical composer whose wider reputation had been secured largely through gramophone recordings – but while Shostakovich did not enjoy the patronage of CBS, he must have been aware that his own international reputation was once again secure. The previous year, his Symphony No 4, a dark and disturbing work which contains some of the loudest music ever written, had at last been premiered in the USSR, almost thirty years after its completion, having been withdrawn in rehearsal. A matter of three months before Stravinksy's visit, with its celebratory concert series, Shostakovich himself had been the subject of an important retrospective in Edinburgh.

So why in that photograph with MacDiarmid and Stevenson does his expression still seem so pessimistic and occluded? Perhaps because the first performance of his Twelfth Symphony had been greeted with such dismay, hailed as his worst major score and damned for its lurid repetitions and crudities. Stevenson suggests that, during that visit to Scotland at least, Shostakovich seemed utterly, self-denyingly absorbed in his music and in its correct performance – faster, always faster. He resembled a "lightning conductor", channeling immense forces in an unexpectedly passive way. When they met in Moscow six years later, there was a lighter side to their conversation, a shared interest in football and the respective merits of Glasgow Rangers and Moscow Dynamo. There are other potential explanations. While Shostakovich presumably no longer feared the midnight knock on the door that would signal his anonymous demise – there was a running joke in pre-war Russia about the "little suitcase" everyone kept packed and ready against that moment – he still lived under the strictest monitoring and was still able to generate enormous controversy. He had been elected as delegate to the Supreme Soviet of the USSR in May, and was already First Secretary of the RSFSR Composers' Union, something which required him, at last, to join the Communist Party, but even then Shostakovitch was still subject to ferocious strictures. His Symphony No 13 would be premiered in December, to the storm of criticism he must have expected. Eight days later, he attended the premiere in Leningrad of his opera *Katerina Ismailova*, a politically "correct" revision of the 1932 work *Lady Macbeth of Mtsensk*, which despite its popular success had called down the wrath of Stalin. Somewhere in between, Shostakovitch married his mistress Irina Supinskaya, but there is no sign of happiness in that Edinburgh photograph, still less in the surviving newsreel footage, which proves that his expression isn't simply a stilted moment in an otherwise relaxed meeting.

The other factor that bore on Shostakovitch was the same that had troubled him in 1949. He was, quite simply, ill at ease in the West and viscerally resistant to its ways. In the autumn of 1962, Britain was still buzzing in the aftermath of the *Lady Chatterley* trial. How ironic that must have seemed to a man who had been condemned for the "pornographic" elements in his *Lady Macbeth*. The Scottish resonance couldn't have been lost on him, either. Also, he had just taken part in a festival whose most celebrated moment had been the carefully staged appearance of a nude woman at a now infamous writers' congress organised by none other than Sonia Orwell, widow of the man who had created the iconic version of the superpower stand-off. And if the chronological 1984 still seemed far distant, the reality of Shostakovitch's world in 1962 was disturbingly close to that of George Orwell's *Nineteen Eighty-Four*. Thought crime and double think were his everyday realities, not aspects of some dystopian fantasy.

The Edinburgh visit offered a sharp instance of how that worked. The great cellist Mstislav Rostropovich, who was conducting some of his friend's work at the Festival, recalls that at a press conference a reporter asked Shostakovich if he had agreed with the Party's criticism of him in 1948. "Yes, yes, yes", said Shostakovich, "and not only do I agree. I am *grateful* to the Party". A standard line, but the composer then turned to Rostropovich and said angrily "That son of a bitch! How could he dare ask that question? Doesn't he understand that I can't answer it?"

And as if to prove how shallow – or utopian – all the talk of peace had been in 1949, mere weeks after his visit to Edinburgh, and only days after Stravinsky returned to the US, an American U2 spy plane returned incontrovertible evidence of a Soviet military build-up, including medium range nuclear missiles, on what President John F Kennedy called the "imprisoned island" of Cuba. The world was plunged into a crisis that threatened all-out atomic war. There were whispers of a power struggle in the Kremlin, a sharp reminder of the old days of ruthless factionalism. The Kennedy brothers wavered, listening to the advice of hawks and doves. American submarines and service ships slipped their moorings in a Scottish loch and put quietly out to sea. For nearly two weeks, the whole world lived under the kind of apocalyptic cloud that had been Shostakovich's lot all his adult life. Questions about political rightness or wrongness looked set to vanish in a rhetorical cloud, mushroom-shaped.

Few modern artists more completely represent the contradictions of the age: politically, aesthetically, psychologically. Inevitably, much nonsense has been written about him, much of it politically inspired, much of it masking a sadder and still more remarkable reality. At the peace conference in 1949, someone else was able to observe him at close quarters. Where Robert Craft later was an American visiting Russia, the composer Nicolai Nabokov was a Russian-born exile in the United States. He sat close alongside Shostakovich and witnessed the same nervous behaviour Craft had noted, twitching, shredding the filters of his cigarettes, symptoms of deep unease and a sharp contrast to the stony-faced impassivity of the other Soviet delegates. "To me", wrote Nabokov in his memoir *Bagazh*, "he seemed like a trapped man, whose only wish was to be left alone, to the peace of his own art and to the tragic destiny to which he, like most of his countrymen, had been forced to resign himself".

History will not let Shostakovich alone, in death any more than in life. Between his death in 1975, when the second edition of Nabokov's memoir was published, until now, his centenary year, there has been a flood of biographical and critical writing, favourable, critical, revisionist, counter-revisionist, and even, in the hall of mirrors called postmodernism, counter-counter-revisionist. It has become customary to begin any new account of Shostakovich's life with some version of "the Volkov affair" and some conclusion about the reliability or otherwise of *Testimony*. I have preferred to leave such a discussion to my final chapter, where it belongs, and to use it as a source when its narrative relevance seems unambiguous. Nor have I assumed that *Testimony* is the crux to any understanding of Shostakovich, his life and his work. That seems to me wrong-headed in the circumstances, which are exceptional. Instead, I have tried to provide a straightforward narrative of the composer's life and the evolution of his music. Our instinctive critical paradigms suggest these two courses should describe a relatively smooth trajectory. Naivety gives way to mature wisdom, obscurity to recognition; "influence" reverses polarity as the susceptibilities of youth are transcended and the artist begins to transmit his own language to subsequent generations. Death – with or without a prior disillusionment and decline – marks the end.

And yet, life-and-work, and still more, life-and-times are only awkwardly twinned in even the most tranquil of lives. More than most creative geniuses, Shostakovich refuses to fit the paradigm. His genius was highly precocious, his influences overcome with rare speed and confidence. His circumstances were so strange and extreme that his work was not allowed to evolve in an organic way, and was not just acted on but acted on with bizarre capriciousness. If Dmitri Shostakovich had grown up in Geneva – or in New York or Edinburgh – the course of his life would inevitably have been very different, but it would also have lacked the deep absorption in Russia and the profound commitment to the Russian people and their culture that gives the work its only recoverable consistency. Heard in sequence – whether the sequence of composition or of first performance – Shostakovitch's oeuvre can seem confusingly haphazard. How could the composer of the great symphonies also have written the drumbeating *The Fearless Regiments Are On The Move*?

As with most such questions, the rhetorical element is not absolute. There is almost always an external reason that explains Shostakovich's apparent regressions. And it is worth saying that such moments can very easily be found in most creative lives. It is just that with Shostakovitch one is always looking for the figure in the carpet, for a political/psychological dimension that as often misleads as it illuminates. This essay attempts to listen for the deeper pulse of the life and the music, not so much to transcend the unavoidable ironies, duplicities and double games as to set them aside for a moment. Its conclusion is clear; history refuses to let him alone because of unpurged guilt or psychological opacity, but very simply because Dmitri Dmitrievich Shostakovich stands among the very greatest exponents – and perhaps the last great exponent – of what we still uneasily call classical music.

Chapter One

Chapter One

On September 14 1960, the recently appointed First Secretary of the RSFSR Composer's Union delivered an address to an open session. As so often, it was difficult to tell how much of Shostakovitch's discomfort came from the words he was required to read or from sheer nervousness and embarrassment at being dragged into the spotlight, but there was no mistaking the passion with which he delivered one (possibly unscripted) line: "For all that is good in me, I owe a debt to my parents".

Even at that period, it would probably have been circumspect to claim that one had been formed and nurtured in the warm embrace of Soviet Communism, suckled by Mother Russia, raised to manhood by the rigours of dialectical materialism. But perhaps Shostakovich was speaking in code, or with the kind of implicit irony that hovers like smoke around almost all his recorded statements: "For all that is *good* in me...for all the rest – my ideological "errors" and shortcomings, my artistic "failures", this awkward wretch I have become – well, who can be blamed for that? myself? you? the great Soviet state?" But the First Secretary's head had gone back down and he continued to read his text in a passionless monotone.

It is a pity that a decade and a half later, as he signed the manuscript pages of *Testimony* for Solomon Volkov, the 69 year old composer seemed to have so few memories of his mother and father, or of his childhood. Whatever else can be said about what was good in him or ill, almost all that can be said firmly about him, his politics and the wellsprings of his music, can be attributed to his parents.

Dmitri Boleslavovich Shostakovich worked as senior keeper in the St Petersburg Chamber (Palace) of Weights and Measures, which had been founded by Dmitri Mendeleyev, who created the periodic table of elements. He had originally trained in histology, a branch of biology specialising in organic tissues, and it is not precisely clear what was his function at the Chamber. After Mendeleyev's death, the institute was run down and Dmitri Boleslavovich found work as manager at the Rennenkampf estates at Irinovka. He also worked in munitions during the First World War. Politics, though, had chequered his career. The family had only recently returned to the capital after a period of political exile in Siberia. Dmitri Boleslavovich's father had been sent there on suspicion of involvement in the assassination of Alexander II. It was an experience he shared with his wife

Sofia Vasilievna Kokaoulina, whose family had become wealthy through running the Lena mines at Bodaibo in Eastern Siberia, the source of that mythical substance, Russian gold.

Shostakovich's parents Sofia and Dmitri photographed early in their marriage

Those Americans who met Shostakovich in 1949 and were dismayed – even disgusted – by his pasty, pock-marked face and neurasthenic manner may, the more generous ones, have put his condition down to the rigours of the late war. In fact, the young Shostakovich was frequently ill, or more accurately, never entirely well. He suffered lymphatic tuberculosis as a child and was operated on. During the Civil War, when the Allies blockaded the new Bolshevik regime, he suffered severe malnutrition and bouts of tuberculosis. So serious was his situation that while Shostakovich was studying at the conservatory, the director, composer Alexander Glazunov, applied on his behalf for extra rations, not so that a precocious young man could luxuriate in extra food, but quite simply to ensure his survival. There had been happier and more plentiful times, notably the summers spent with his sisters at Irinovka (in photographs "Mitya" looks blissful standing between his sisters) but even before the Revolution everyday life was spartan by Western standards and there was always the additional fear of a visit by the Okhrana, the Tsarist secret police, forerunners of the Cheka, OGPU, NKVD and ultimately KGB of the Soviet years.

The Shostakoviches had some reason to fear such a visit. Before considering the family's political background, it is worth noting that the first twelve years of Dmitri Dmitrievich's life were precisely bracketed by the two Russian revolutions, that of 1905, and then of 1917. Less than two years before his son's birth, Dmitri Boleslavovich was present with his brother-in-law at the infamous Bloody Sunday massacre of January 9 1905, a turning point in Russian history when Tsarist troops fired on a crowd in Palace Square who were protesting about food shortages. His son must have grown up with stories of that terrible day, and he was certainly old enough to have heard news of the Lena massacre. Discontent in the goldfields had come to a head on February 29 1912 when rotten meat was distributed to hungry families by one of the company owned stores. The strike that followed engulfed most of the mines. The strike leaders were arrested at the beginning of April. On the following day, a crowd of 2,500 marched on the Nadezhdinsky goldfield to demand their release. In a tragic echo of Bloody Sunday, troops fired on the crowd; 270 were killed and a further 250 wounded.

One can only imagine the impact this had on Sofia Shostakovich, whose family had been enlightened administrators, committed to improving the workers' conditions. Like her husband, she was a Narodnik, of the people's party, and both were passionately committed to democracy. Their beliefs were shared by other members of the family. Shostakovich's paternal grandfather had been an adherent of Land and Will (*Zemlya i Volya*), a revolutionary group much influenced by Nikolai Chernyshevsky. Several of Shostakovich's uncles and aunts had been active in anti-Tsarist politics before the revolution of 1905; and his mother's sister Nadia, who lived with the family in St Petersburg, was radicalised by Bloody Sunday and became an early Bolshevik, a detail inevitably made much of in official Soviet hagiographies of the composer. On at least one occasion, the family home at ulitsa Podolskaya was raided by Okhrana agents, searching for inflammatory literature. Mercifully, they found none. The fiancé of another aunt, Lyubochka, was arrested on a trumped-up charge of murdering a policeman and freed only with difficulty.

It is hard to exaggerate the impact of this background on the young composer-to-be. It is also important to clear away any illusion that there was a smooth continuum between the two Russian revolutions, that they were simply different aspects of the same process. The revolution of 1905 was populist and democratic, libertarian in its essence. That of 1917 was fiercely centralist and authoritarian, avant-gardist in spirit and totalitarian to the core. All his life Dmitri Shostakovich sustained a passionate and unswerving commitment to the Russian people, their traditions and their self-defining wisdom. It is against that conviction, not his inconsistent and often puzzling reactions to the vagaries of Soviet Communism, not his attitude to Marxism-Leninism or the "science" of dialectical materialism, that all his work has to be judged and understood.

Dmitri Dmitrievich Shostakovich was born in St Petersburg on September 25 1906 (September 12 old style). He was to have been called Jaroslav, but the priest overruled the parents. There was an older sister, Maria, born three years before him; a second daughter, Zoya, was born in 1908.

With Nadia also living in the house and his father much absent, it was women who largely defined him, not unusual for that time and class but profoundly important nonetheless. The first tragedy of Shostakovich's life was the premature death in 1914 of his much-loved aunt Lyubochka. His father's death in 1922, weakened by the hardships of the Civil War, is thought to have cast a tragic pall over much of his son's subsequent work, but it's difficult not to find a tinge of guilty self-pity there as well. Sofia took work as a cashier to keep the family solvent, and Nadia came home from the Urals to boost the ration book with her new husband's special academic allowance. Dmitri was spared the duty of breadwinner for his mother and sisters. Even at that stage, his art was all.

When we describe Shostakovich as a precocious talent, it shouldn't be taken to mean that, like some St Petersburg Mozart, he began writing piano pieces at the age of 3 or 4, or that he had a true prodigy's instinct for performance, picking at the keys as soon as he could reach them. In fact, Shostakovich was a relatively late starter. There is little doubt that his childhood home was full of music. Dmitri Boleslavovich apparently liked to sing *tsigany* or gypsy songs to the accompaniment of his guitar. Nicholas Slonimsky rather optimistically describes Sofia as "a professional pianist". She was, in fact, a teacher and though conservatory trained is probably best considered a very accomplished amateur, much in demand to play at the houses of friends and her husband's colleagues. At first it was assumed that Dmitri would become an engineer like his father, a role that sat well with the Shostakoviches' progressive and meliorist philosophy. Mother Russia needed skilled men.

The first formal musical experience that we know of is a family visit to the opera in 1914, when Dmitri was 8. They saw a production of *The Legend of Tsar Sultan*, which of course includes the famous test piece "Flight of the Bumble Bee". An avid reader, Dmitri may well have known the story already; Pushkin was already a favourite. Whatever he made later in life of Rimsky-Korsakov's "perfumed" music (the description is Neville Cardus's), and it seems the antithesis of his own, it is interesting to note that Shostakovich's Opus 1, a Scherzo written when he was 13, is a homage to Rimsky. It is reasonable to suppose that he would have shared Cardus's wry opinion that the idea of Rimsky revising the work of Shostakovitch's revered Mussorgsky, who for him encapsulated the soul and spirit of old Russia, was a little like having Swinburne revise Robert Burns.

Not until the following year, when the war in the East had settled to its own brutal stalemate, did Sofia persuade Dmitri to sit at the piano and practise some simple scales. What followed does perhaps merit terms like precocity or even genius. The boy seemed to absorb music like oxygen. His progress was disconcertingly rapid. Bored with academic exercises, he quickly outgrew his first teacher Ignati Gliasser and outdistanced his classmates. Private lessons with Alexandra Rozanova were more fruitful.

All Dmitri's diffidence and awkwardness disappeared when at the piano. Someone who saw him perform at a family friend's house commented: "The skinny boy is transformed into a bold musician with a man's strength and captivating rhythmic drive". By the age of 10, he had mastered a considerable repertoire.

There was another important development, which saw the B-A-C-H motto progressively to evolve into D-S-C-H. Dull as Gliasser's teaching may have been, it did not extinguish the creative spark. Shostakovich's first known composition has not survived and there is no reason to think that *The Soldier (Ode to Liberty),* a piano piece, was anything other than a rather conventional expression of wartime sentiment but it was a sign of things to come (and cheerfully gives the lie to any suggestion that Shostakovitch only wrote patriotic works at the command of his Soviet masters).

Sometime in 1917 he also wrote a *Funeral March for the Victims of the Revolution.* The piece was subsequently destroyed, but its main theme was to be a revenant, hauntingly repeated in the opening movement of the Symphony No 2 and heard once again 35 years later in the closing movement of the Symphony No 12. What dents the seeming orthodoxy of their respective dedications, *To October* and *The Year 1917,* is the knowledge that the original piece was inspired by the sight of a young boy hacked to death by a Cossack on the Letny Prospekt, when Shostakovich was 10, apparently for stealing an apple. There may have been little continuity between the ideals of 1905 and the brutal reality of October 1917, but in Shostakovich's mind there was scant moral differentiation between the victims of Tsarist repression and the later victims of Communist terror. The change of calendar meant that the Revolution was actually located in November, but the original date stuck. "October" may have briefly stood as an emblem of liberty – the overthrow of the Tsar was hailed by all shades of political opinion as signalling a potential revolution in human nature – but Shostakovitch could only look back on 1917 with deep ambivalence. Official Soviet biographies placed the 11 year old Dmitri at the Finland Station in April of that fateful year, allegedly watching the arrival of V I Lenin in his sealed train. Shostakovich himself either could not remember the moment or feigned forgetfulness, about his glimpse of the "tyrant", but all his life he carried with him something that had happened the year before, the flash of a sabre and young blood suddenly spilt.

So impressive was Dmitri's progress that in 1919 he was enrolled at Petrograd Conservatoire (the city's name had been changed five years earlier to something less German, more Russian sounding; not until 1924 was it renamed Leningrad) as its youngest matriculated student. He studied piano with Leonid Nikolayev, but in the autumn was allowed to join Maximilian Steinberg's composition class, having taken some private composition lessons in the summer. Steinberg was the son-in-law of Rimsky-Korsakov, who had died when Shostakovitch was two, and so that early Scherzo may have been as much flattery of a teacher as a genuine homage to the older composer. (Three years later, Shostakovich did orchestrate Rimsky's *I Watched For Thee in the Grotto.*)

He made rapid progress at the Conservatoire, watched over by director Glazunov, who managed to survive the Bolshevik Revolution and stayed in post for a further difficult decade. Though devoted to all his pupils, Glazunov took an especially paternalistic interest in the boy's progress, which may well have reminded him of his own prodigious youth. Notwithstanding the slightly sour and sardonic comments about the older man in *Testimony* (one of that strange

ДМИТРИЙ ДМИТРИЕВИЧ ШОСТАКОВИЧ

Photographed on a garden bench at 18 Dmitri Shostakovich had already mastered the direct and unblinking gaze that would become his trademark expression.

book's troubling false notes) Shotakovitch had much reason to be grateful. In 1920, Glazunov made him an award from the Borodin Fund for young composers. Two years later, following a first attack of malnutrition, he was granted extra rations by commissar Anatoli Lunacharsky, again at Glazunov's behest.

If the "signature" of a piano composer's work is almost always conditioned by the size and shape of his hands – Ferrucio Busoni and Rachmaninov were both big men and their work reflects it – it's clear from Shostakovich's keyboard output that he did not possess the most generous stretch in the fingers. Fated by both genes and circumstance to be short in stature, he was seriously myopic and his health was further undermined by Civil War shortages. The sudden death of his father in February 1922 was a further blow, in which grief and self-interest both played a part. It looked very much as though Shostakovich might have to give up his studies and find work to support the family. Sofia, though, found work as a cashier, while Maria, who had recently completed her piano diploma, found work as an accompanist at the College of Choreography.

The family's circumstances were still precarious, however. Over the next two years, Shostakovich was obliged to seek work at the Bright Reel and other cinemas, most pressingly when Sofia contracted malaria in the spring of 1924. By then, Shostakovich had himself undergone a further bout of severe ill-health, diagnosed as tuberculosis, which had necessitated an expensive convalescence at Koreiz, a sanatorium in the Crimea (arranged by Glazunov, of course). There were, however, upsides to both experiences. Playing live accompaniment to silent films, and at a moment when cinema was seen as the cutting edge of Soviet culture, was a bracing immersion in the *Zeitgeist*; it expanded Shostakovitch's expressive range considerably, and reinforced in him a musical naturalism that had both satiric-comic and tragical dimensions. In addition, the Crimean sojourn threw him together with his first fiancée. The sixth, seventh and eighth of the *Preludes* written in the early months of 1920 had been dedicated to Natasha Kuba, who is identified as the boy's first girlfriend; the other pieces in the sequence were dedicated to Maria (numbers two to five) with the first dedicated to Boris Kustodiev, who painted the 13 year old Shostakovich's portrait that summer. In the Crimea, though, he met and quickly became engaged to Tanya Glivenko, the daughter of a Moscow philologist who seems to have held some trustee capacity in the running of the sanatorium which allowed him to place Tanya and her sister there for the summer.

It is hard to imagine the awkward and obsessive Dmitri being swept away by an affair of the heart, but he seems to have been captivated by the girl. Even so, it is difficult to judge whether, now that his piano studies were complete, his wish to move to Moscow to study composition under that ardent symphonist Nikolai Myaskovsky (Shostakovich's eventual 15 hardly matches Myaskovsky's 37) was a considered career move or simply a desire to be close to Tanya. In the event, his mother intervened, he was persuaded to stay in Petrograd and complete his composition training with Steinberg. But the engagement continued for some six years, and even after Tanya had married someone else, it seemed not impossible that she would leave her husband and return to Shostakovich. Only after the birth of her child did he accept the inevitable and marry Nina Vasilyevna Varzar. Not for the last time in his life did that unprepossessing exterior conceal a roil of competing passions. Shotakovich's emotional life was, if anything, more complex than his politics.

The Op 8 Piano Trio in C minor was dedicated to Tanya but it was also his application piece for the free class at the Moscow Conservatoire. Though fresher and less dense than his later writing – he was only 16 after all – it certainly does not sound like the work of a young man in love. The opening is a falling melody line that gradually builds up over a heavy, repetitive figure, hinting at the grotesquerie that was to disturb Steinberg but was to become a defining characteristic of Shostakovich's music for much of his life. There is also an unexpected hint of Rachmaninov in the piano writing, a surprise given his apparent later dislike of that composer. However, it is hardly unusual to detect the anxiety of influence in a young composer. The miracle is how quickly Shostakovich assimilated and transcended his. There were plenty more pressing anxieties in store.

The loss of his father had been a grievous blow, but probably the worst outcome for the ambitious young composer of the family's recent misfortunes and his own ill-health was the suspension of work on the symphony he had finished drafting around the beginning of 1923. This was the form in which his essence as a composer would be expressed, an essence characterised by unflinching musical dialectic, a never ending contention between formality and chaos, and a sharp duality of tragedy and satiric farce. It can, and has, been argued that the symphonies represent the "public" Shostakovich, the work of a masked man, while the chamber music expresses the "private" Shostakovich. It seems a false dichotomy, not because the great cycle of string quartets, only begun in 1938, is not intensely expressive inscape in the manner of late Beethoven, later of Béla Bartók and the "autobiographical" string quartet writing of Leoš Janáček and Bedřich Smetana, but because the symphonies are quintessentially personal too, even when in them Shostakovich seems to be playing a curious, possibly even duplicitous role.

In between these imagined poles lies the piano music, inevitably personal because written for his own instrument, but also inherently public because it was the most immediate vehicle for Shostakovich's performing self. From the grief-stricken Op 6 Suite in F# for two pianos written in memory of his father in 1923 to the great Bachian sequence of Twenty-Four Preludes, Op 34, finished in 1933, the piano music also represents the full spectrum of his compositional personality. There is another reason for its importance. While the teenage Shostakovitch dreamed of joining Myaskovsky in Moscow and of writing symphonies, he was very much the product of a virtual obsession with piano music and performance imposed on the St Petersburg Conservatoire by its founder Anton Rubinstein. Seen as the only real rival among piano virtuosi to Franz Liszt, Rubinstein hid his own own flagrant disregard for the notes as written behind a great wave of passionate "expression", but in further guilty compensation insisted on accuracy as an absolute standard for Conservatoire students. Peter Ilyich Tchaikovsky was one of his first significant students. It was a curious relationship: Tchaikovsky worshipped him, Rubinstein disliked his pupil. His more secure legacy was introducing the great European classics to American audiences in a series of money-spinning tours, permanently transforming musical tastes in the United States and arguably paving the way for Shostakovich's brief lionisation during the war.

However much a product of the Rubinstein establishment, and however much the present directorate insisted that his natural path was as a pianist/composer in the Lisztian mould, Dmitri was convinced that the symphony was his natural means of expression.

The late winter of 1924 was to be Lenin's last. His death in January signalled the start of an inexorable change in Soviet politics, marked by internecine squabbling over the succession and the future course of international Communism; it also marked the beginning of the slow, dialectical transformation of "Leninism" into its even darker sibling "Stalinism", the perverse and intermittently vicious political methodology that would haunt the remainder of Shostakovich's life. The opposition of heroic Lenin and totalitarian Stalin is, of course, a Western myth, but Shostakovich and his fellow-students had an immediate and ironic reminder of what had changed in the renaming of his city and its conservatoire to Leningrad.

He resumed work on his symphonic sketches in October of that year. The family was still in hardship. Sofia was ill and exhausted and Dmitri would continue to work as a cinema pianist until February of the following year when three of his works (including the finished symphony and the Op11a Prelude for string octet, which was dedicated to his dead friend Volodya Kurchavov) were published. Shostakovich broke off work on his symphony to write a memorial to the young poet. That was not the only interruption. The previous month Sofia had been violently mugged outside her apartment block. Despite these setbacks, Shostakovich worked doggedly and on July 1 1925 finished the score.

The Symphony No 1 in F minor, Op 10 was submitted and accepted for Shostakovich's composition diploma. It represents a brave and exceptional symphonic debut, far removed from the respectful homages and spring-like optimism that characterises most first symphonies. For a start, the work divides into two large blocks of radically different character. If there are strong influences at work – and it almost seems too acute and individual for that – they are Stravinsky (and particularly *Petrushka*) in the opening two movements, and the tragic world of Tchaikovsky in the final two. This is a work that may begin in the present, but seems to end facing the past. The opening section alternates a march and a delicate waltz first heard on flute and woodwinds. There are early hints of the martial irruptions which seem to represent the Nazi invaders in the wartime symphonies, or the forces of reaction and repression in the other, ostensibly historically based works. Here, though, they seem to be little more than exercises in the dramatic tension, timbre and dynamic, though it's puzzling why a composer of Shostakovich's precocious talent should not have found a way to resolve such contentious material rather than simply stepping away from it. Perhaps something darker is betokened, even under such a playful surface.

The second movement is a true Scherzo, again almost skittishly surreal. Significantly, it is the piano's first entrance that imposes some kind of order and sense of pupose on the material. Vivid orchestral outbreaks are interrupted by a songful Trio just as they seem to be going somewhere, and then the first surprise...One commentator has likened the aural impact to the composer crumpling his score in disgust. Three vicious piano chords seem to call a halt to proceedings. The lower strings make a disgruntled response and then three further chords – Stravinskian in dramatic effect – bring the movement to a sharp end.

Something fundamental has happened. If one looks for a thematic explanation, the opening of the Lento perhaps signifies childhood's end, or perhaps the fading of political hope. The mood now seems unrelievedly pessimistic and brooding. Oboe and cello try to find some relief, but again there is a blunt opposition between a fiercely martial section (trumpet and war drums) and further humane calls from oboe, clarinet and violin. Again, the material does not so much reach a conclusion as simply disembody.

The stage is thereby set for an upbeat and affirmative Finale. It is, instead, blunt and disorderly, indifferent in every way to further woodwind calls. Piano again helps to impose some kind of structure and the first great melody in Shostakovich's work slowly emerges, most distinctly stated by solo violin. The music builds in power and authority until it comes hard up against the fatalistic conclusion of the Lento movement, restated *fortissimo* on the kettledrums, but this time in the form of a question. There is some attempt to provide a response, but the weight of the military figure is now too strong and it brings the symphony to a darkly chastened conclusion.

With hindsight, and according to one's preference for a strictly technical over a psychological interpretation, there are many ways of judging the First Symphony: as a bold technical exercise that could not be maintained, or which might seem too bold in a diploma piece to be tactically sound; as a sharp rejection of modernist ironies (those mechanistic themes and procedures in the first two movements) and retreat into history; as a strikingly honest representation of Shostakovich's own recent experience, youthful irresponsibility pulled up short by bereavement, hunger, hard work, and intimations of his own mortality; it can also be read as a parable of recent Russian history, or rather a reverse parable, with the forces of collectivism having to face up to an inexorable fate, a kind of return-of-the-repressed.

As so often with Shostakovich, the work is capacious enough to sustain any number of contradictory interpretations. What is immediately clear is that the young composer is in complete command of his material, even when he appears not to be, and that he has a clear understanding of its perverse trajectory. Glazunov immediately recognised its quality and arranged to have the work performed. Shostakovich himself may have drawn equal satisfaction from being able to travel to Moscow to play a piano reduction of the score for Myaskovsky, but exactly a fortnight earlier, on May 12 1926 Nikolai Malko conducted the premiere in St Petersburg.

For all its callow contradictions of tone, the work was an immediate hit with critics and audiences. Shostakovich took four curtain calls at the first performance. Not for another eight years, with the premiere of his opera *Lady Macbeth of Mtsensk*, would Shostakovich enjoy a similar success. On that later occasion, though, the victory would be pyrrhic and would mark the real beginning of his bizarre and troubled relationship with the man who had picked up the dead Lenin's torch and taken obsessive charge of every aspect of Soviet politics and culture. The public may have enjoyed Shostakovich's opera, but Joseph Stalin loathed it, and the leader's critical disapproval could be fatal.

Когда я ночью жду ее прихода,
Жизнь, кажется, висит на волоске.
Что почести, что юность, что свобода
Пред милой гостьей с дудочкой в руке.
И вот вошла. Откинув покрывало,
Внимательно взглянула на меня.
Ей говорю: "Ты ль Данту диктовала
Страницы Ада?" Отвечает: "Я"

Chapter Two

Chapter Two

When Shostakovich died in 1975, almost half a century after the brilliant première of his Symphony No 1, the Soviet government put out a statement hailing his work as "a remarkable example of fidelity to the traditions of musical classicism". The communique lapses into more familiar rhetoric thereafter, mentioning Shostakovich's contributions to "socialist realism", his unflinchingly realistic approach to Russian life and traditions, and his contribution to "universal progressive musical culture". However ironically it may have sounded, given the many tendentious issues that surrounded his work, and all the critical vagaries that greeted it, the first part of that statement cannot be faulted.

It is already possible, even this early in the story, to offer a general description of Shostakovich's music. Without any doubt few great artists in any form have shown such consistency of purpose. It is not a career that divides easily into "periods", other than those dictated by external circumstance, and while there is inevitably considerable variation between Shostakovich's writing between and within different genres – string quartets, piano music, vocal music and opera, the symphony – all of it, nearly 150 separate opus numbers, is driven by the same adamantine logic. "Fidelity" and "classicism" may seem curious words to find in an official Soviet statement, but they are absolutely pertinent.

Shostakovich was fated to be dismissed as old-fashioned by Western critics in thrall to the modernism of the Second Viennese School, and by his countrymen as suspiciously new-fangled. He was to a degree Janus-faced, not in his political sympathies, which remained constant, but in his simultaneous modernity and traditionalism. Though he dabbled later with elements of the dodecaphonic approach once condemned as anti-musical, they were fiercely circumscribed by classical tonality; the Twelfth String Quartet and his final symphony, the Fifteenth, both use a tone-row but are in D flat and in C major, the key of classical affirmation, respectively. Unlike Stravinsky, who went through a "serialist" period, influenced by his American amanuensis Craft, Shostakovich was rigorously tonal in approach. He made free use of the violently dissonant harmonies that had become part of the language of 20th century music, but only in such a way that answered the harmonic teleology of the defining key signature. Much of the violent drama and acerbic satire heard in his work is actually the function of easily identi-

Concentrating on his score Shostakovich is photographed at his desk in 1943

DMITRI DMITRIEVICH SHOSTAKOVICH

This iconic photograph of Shostakovich, in wartime in a fireman's uniform, was used across the world as a propaganda image

Дмитрий Дмитриевич Шостакович

fied musical procedures and does not need any extraneous explanation. And yet, from his second symphony onward, Shostakovich's work was subjected to intense non-musical scrutiny, its themes, message, tone, literalness or sarcasm, sincerity or artifice argued over with rare ferocity.

Before considering the Second Symphony, it is worth pausing for a moment to consider the comments of two other distinguished composers. At the height of Shostakovich's fame in 1944, Arnold Schoenberg wrote to Kurt List, editor of *Listen: The Guide to Good Music* in New York, thanking him for copies of articles about himself and about Shostakovich. The implication is that the latter was at least in part negative, for Schoenberg seems to jump to the Russian's defence, following his thanks with "though I still think Shostakovich is a great talent. It is perhaps not his fault that he has allowed politics to influence his compositorial style. And even if it is a weakness in his character – he might be no hero, but a talented musician. In fact, there are heroes, and there are composers. Heroes can be composers and vice versa, but you cannot require it".

At the height of the war against Hitler and fascism – Schoenberg was writing from his distant exile in California – Shostakovich had been pressed into service as both. The helmeted fireman who wrote the Seventh Symphony was understood to be a powerful spokesman for his country's political ideals and chief musical celebrant of its historical achievements. Schoenberg's comment – "a weakness in his character" – has been echoed down the years in line with the assumption that Shostakovich willingly or at best self-protectively subordinated his art to the service of the Union of Soviet Socialist Republics and its rapidly changing policies.

Here, though, is another comment about Shostakovich from a distinguished fellow-musician. Though it relates to a much later work, it has profound bearing on all of Shostakovich's work from the Second Symphony onward. British composer Michael Tippett's longevity makes it easy to forget that he was a near contemporary of the great Russian – Tippett was born in January 1905 and died in 1998 – while the anthropological obsessions of his operas and the pictorial elegance of late works like *The Rose Lake* obscure the committed leftism of his earlier years. Though resistant to dogma, the young Tippett was a socialist through and through, so his perspective on Shostakovitch is worth canvassing. As quoted by his companion and amanuensis Meirion Bowen, Tippett mentions that the Eleventh Symphony "is supposed to be concerned with the events of the 1905 revolution. I was quite sure when I heard it that the use of 1905 *was a kind of political alibi,* since this was a matter of known revolutionary history. The music to me *was self-evidently about Shostakovich's own experiences in the catastrophe of his life*".

Therein lie the key questions that go to the root of Shostakovich's life and work. In what sense was it a "catastrophe"? And what do we understand by "meaning" in instrumental or orchestral music? And specifically political meaning? Can we talk about "subject"? Must a work that bears a poetic title be heard differently to one that merely carries an opus number? How do verbal and musical meaning relate? Or what can we infer from the juxtaposition of certain words and certain sounds? And underneath it all, how do we excavate the composer's "real" intention?

The year 1927 marked an epoch in Soviet Communism and in Shostakovich's life. In October, against all odds, Russians celebrated the tenth anniversary of the Bolshevik Revolution. The regime had survived civil war, foreign intervention, famine, various "counter-revolutionary" initiatives internally, and a fierce power struggle that would lead to the expulsion of Leon Trotsky and Grigori Zinoviev and the introduction of Stalin's nationalist programme of "socialism in one country".

Exactly one week before the United Opposition was purged, on November 5, Shostakovich's Symphony No 2 in B Op 14 was premiered in Leningrad. It was a time of profound change for the young composer. He had been accepted for a higher degree and would remain a postgraduate student until July 1928. He had, some months before, destroyed his juvenilia, a conventional enough gesture, but a clear sign that he now had a clear image of what kind of composer he wanted to become. In April 1927, he met the brilliant, seemingly omniscient Ivan Sollertinsky, who was to become arguably the closest friend of his life and a significant intellectual influence. He also met the woman who would become his first wife, Nina Varzar, the daughter of well-off parents and a natural philosophy student; their engagement came two years later.

Shostakovich's personal horizons seemed to be widening. As he took a break from composition following the success of the First Symphony, he began to spread his wings as a performer. The only major piece written in this period was, significantly, a virtuosic keyboard work, the fiendish Piano Sonata No 1 Op 12. At the end of January, shortly after premiering the sonata in Moscow, he had performed in the First International Chopin Competition in Warsaw. Though he didn't win, the subsequent tour took him through Poland and to Berlin, where he met the conductor Bruno Walter, an important champion of his work in Europe, as Leopold Stokowski was to be in America. In November, Walter conducted the First Symphony in Berlin. Just over two weeks earlier, Shostakovich's Symphony No 2 in B was premiered in Leningrad.

It is immediately and strikingly different from its predecessor. It is, for a start, written in a single movement, but more intriguingly it, for the first time, bears a programmatic title and concludes on a choral part with text. Where the First Symphony is usually analysed on technical and structural grounds, the question of meaning, of the composer's non-musical intentions and affiliations now seems to arise, inescapably but misleadingly. As a title *To October* seems conventional enough for a Soviet composer of the time – Eisenstein's film *October* was being shown around the same time – and the choral text could not be more conventionally affirmative. By 1927, the Marxist mantra "Proletarians of all countries, unite!", which is also affixed to the script, was as ubiquitous and unconsidered as "Drink Coca-Cola" in the West. Revisionist biographers and critics have tried to suggest that Shostakovich's title – he had apparently also considered calling the Piano Sonata *October Symphony* – does not refer specifically to the Bolshevik Revolution but to a more abstract spirit of democracy and a promise of freedom which Shos-

*An early photograph of Shostakovich with his first wife Nina Varzar and his
close friend Ivan Sollertinsky*

takovich already considered to be betrayed. To be sure, his political sympathies were more fully engaged by the revolution of 1905, to which the Eleventh Symphony was dedicated. (Interestingly, the poet and novelist Boris Pasternak, whose career in some measure parallels Shostakovich's, but who was then very much a favoured writer, chose the occasion of the tenth anniversary of the Bolshevik ascendancy to mark *The Year 1905*.) To some extent, such titles are gestural. Almost every writer, artist and musician in the Soviet Union was producing texts that invoked revolutionary history and spirit, and the Second Symphony was written on commission from Muzsektor, overseen by Stalin's Enlightenment commissar Lunacharsky. It may be that at 21, Shostakovich liked the idea of being a composer-laureate to the new regime, and was prepared to subordinate his own convictions to Communist rhetoric. Or, it may have been the composer's first tentative step towards constructing the creative "alibi" Tippett refers to, camouflaging a private drama with public gestures.

Whether the words are Shostakovich's own, or Solomon Volkov's clever ventriloquism, there is a passage in *Testimony* which precisely addresses the question of meaning in music and sets it in the broadest cultural context. Shostakovich concedes that the issue might sound strange to someone raised in the West: "It's here in Russia that the question is usually posed: What was the composer trying to say, after all, with this musical work? What was he trying to make clear? The questions are naive, of course, but despite their naivete and crudity, they definitely merit being asked. And I would add to them, for instance: Can music attack evil? Can it make man stop and think?..." When, in 1936, Shostakovich vociferously denied the then-routine charge of "Formalism", it was less on personal grounds than from a deep, almost genetic conviction that art conceived purely as form and without some moral content was a chimera. Long before "Stalinism" or "Socialist Realism" there was a deep didactic strain in Russian art. After all, Lenin's pamphlet *What Is To Be Done?* takes its title directly from a 19th century novel by Chernyshevsky. The political reliability or otherwise of the intellectuals – a principle known as *(ne)blagonadyozhny* – had been an obsessive issue since the reign of Catherine the Great. That context in no way invalidates Tippett's suggestion that Shostakovich used politics as a kind of front; though Russian to the depths of his soul, he also understood that art was also the expression of a soul, and not some abstract collectivity. There, and not in Communism-vs-anti-Communism, lies the paradox of Dmitri Shostakovich.

The Second Symphony is a strange work not because it bears a "political" or "historical" subtext but because its music is strange. It is, in reality, a cantata, subsequently renamed as a symphony. Its self-consciousness is (to borrow the infamous superscription of the Fifth Symphony, written a decade later) the creative reply of a Soviet artist to just, or unjust, criticism. That may very well explain why in later years Shostakovich effectively disclaimed it, along with the Third; he asked his son Maxim for a promise not to conduct either work. The criticism came from within the new Soviet cultural establishment. The Russian Association of Proletarian Musicians had, in a sour foretaste of what was to come in the 1930s, criticised the

First Symphony's dependence on the romantic individualism of Tchaikovsky and other "bourgeois" composers. The westward-looking, rival Association of Contemporary Musicians warned that he ran the risk of seeming out of date.

In response, Shostakovich wrote a work that is almost onomatopoeically responsive to the times. It is hard to recover the atmosphere of post-revolutionary Russia. The Western caricature of Russia and Russians as dour, unsmiling, ascetic, slavishly obedient to authority is little more than that, or no more than an extrapolation from later circumstances. For a period in the 1920s, a hectic moral anarchy reigned, more libertine than libertarian. The overthrow of bourgeois authority stretched into private life – sexual freedom was preached, divorce and abortion sanctioned – and ultimately into art as well. Experimentalism was all. "Biomechanics" was the fashionable retort to romantic love, altruism, principled action; we are as machines, it proclaims, as driven as any industrial engine or motor car; reason is an illusion. Poet Vladimir Mayakovsky, a kind of literary punk happy to parrot official anathema and spit vitriol at more talented figures, became the darling of the Revolution, and in turn the most prominent victim of the cycle of favour and disfavour. In 1929, Shostakovich wrote incidental music for his play *The Bedbug*, a critical disaster. After the further failure of *The Bathhouse* the following spring, Mayakovsky shot himself. It was a symbolic end to the old decade. His rehabilitation by Stalin as the "greatest...most gifted" just five years later was just one of the perversities of the new one.

The Second Symphony is not a field recording, but it captures a mood with disconcerting precision. Almost entirely abstract and themeless, it studiously avoids the expressive inscape and tragic conclusion of the First Symphony. It tells no story, unless the wild juxtaposition of separate lines is intended to reflect the ideological morass out of which the Party rose, triumphant and strong. Or, in the inevitable alternative view, do those same passages reflect the wild amorality and unregulated self-definition that *followed* the Revolution, however briefly? There is no answer, just as there is no way of making an absolute judgement about the work's apparently dominant influence. If Stravinsky and Tchaikovsky respectively stood over the two halves of the First Symphony, its successor seems haunted by the work of Alexander Scriabin (1872-1915), who had recently and posthumously – Scriabin died in 1915, aged just 41 – been declared sound and affirmative by Lunacharsky. Is that the point? Was Shostakovitch kow-towing to official tastes and prescriptions? Or was he sarcastically celebrating a composer whose "mystic chords", theatrical aura and theosophical pretensions Shostakovich instinctively despised?

A bleak slow passage for strings follows and then there is a restatement, on clarinet, of the theme from the youthful *Funeral March for the Victims of the Revolution*. This high part, an atonal fugato, is the only clear-cut thematic writing in the entire work, and will appear again in the Twelfth Symphony, with its dedication to *The Year 1917*. The deep structure of Shostakovich's musical imagination starts to reveal itself.

And then, the choir comes in, singing of Lenin and struggle, the forging of a destiny out of despair. It's hard to hear the finale as anything other than Bolshevik propaganda. Shostakovich, of course, did not write the words, professed to loathe them and treats them with curious disregard in his setting. The text was given to him by Alexander Bezymensky, writer-in-residence with TRAM, the Leningrad Working Youth Theatre; in return, Shostakovich agreed to act as musical director. As ever, it isn't clear which came first. Given the literary associations he was making, and which would soon impact strongly on his life and career, one would have thought he could have found a more distinguished text. On the other hand, Shostakovich was pressed for time and always aware of Muzsektor watching over his shoulder for any signs of bourgeois self-indulgence.

There is a simple, knot-cuttting explanation for Shostakovich's later disavowal of the Second Symphony: it is not very good. Like many artists who achieve success with their first major work – one thinks of the young American novelist he met in New York in 1949 who struggled to equal the success of *The Naked and the Dead* – Shostakovich seemed emptied out and directionless. Such a man is clearly susceptible to external influences, particularly if they carry a certain promise of professional security. Such factors notwithstanding, Shostakovich seemed to be going through a transformation, not sloughing a skin, but adding a new and impenetrable one.

He returned to symphonic writing two years later, and rattled off his Symphony No 3 in E flat, Op 20 in less than a month. Unlike the Second Symphony, it was not written to a commission. Like its predecessor, though, it is a single movement work with a historical subtitle *The First of May* and a choral finale, this time after a poem by Semyon Kirsanov. It has the same vocalised quality and the same *audio-verite* impression of shouting voices, milling crowds, a mixture of hectic enthusiasm and deep dread. Ian MacDonald, a shrewd observer of Shostakovich suggests that the first aural intimations of nemesis can be heard in the work. If so, there is an irony in the circumstances of its creation, for Shostakovich finished his score while staying at a Black Sea resort in Georgia, only a score or so *versts* distant from the birthplace of Joseph Vissarionovich Djugashvili. the one-time brigand who now ran the Soviet Union under his revolutionary soubriquet. Whether one really can hear "the Man of Steel" in the clanking brass and rumbling strings of the Third Symphony is a less interesting question than where one locates Dmitri Shostakovich in it. It is, at least on the surface, an orthodox Communist symphony, written at the composer's own behest and under no apparent duress. Whether it is something else below the surface is the moot point.

MacDonald also cites the perceptive English critic Gerald Abraham, who in *Eight Soviet Composers* describes his inescapable feeling, listening to the Third Symphony, that Shostakovich "is playing a part...He tries to be Marxian, but fantastic Gogolian humour keeps breaking in". This is doubly perceptive. It underscores MacDonald's central thesis about Shostakovich, and Michael Tippett's: that he donned a self-protective armour of apparent orthodoxy and compliance through the chinks in which one senses an array of contradictory emotions and attitudes – satire, rancour, self-pity, self-aggrandizement, harsh laughter, pathos, an irrepressible human-ism, all the way to overt *anti*-Communism. Sarcastic overstatement – or *vranyo* – is a favourite Russian rhetorical device. Where, say, a French anti-clerical writer might launch a frontal assault on the Church, replete with exaggerated accusa-tions of simony, greed, drunkenness and sexual perversion, a Russian would be more inclined to subvert religious or secular authority by an affectation of absurd piety or orthodoxy. Perhaps Shostakovich's "Communist" hymns and paeans are exaggerated with satiric intent.

Something else, even more profoundly subversive, may be at work. Mac-Donald, Solomon Volkov, and by implication, Abraham all persuasively align Shostakovich with the ancient principle of *yurodstvo*. MacDonald's summary can-not be bettered: "The *yurodivy* or 'holy fool' is a venerable Russian tradition whereby anyone wishing to mock the mighty may do so with relative impunity *provided they behave in all other aspects as if unworthy of serious attention* [my ital-ics]. The parallel with the English court jester is more or less exact and it is sig-nificant that the Fool in *King Lear* was, after Hamlet, Shostakovich's favourite Shakespearian creation". Much has been made of Shostakovich's resemblance to Hamlet, his prevarication, procrastination, self-doubt, even his affectation of in-sanity when he seemed to dare the Claudius-like Soviet regime. It is an analogy that broke down somewhat when the Nazi Fortinbras was battering at the Rus-sian gates. Was he any more the Fool? The trap for Shostakovich lay in that impor-tant qualification italicised above. Had he passed his career writing satirical songs to be sung in bars or in drawing rooms, like his father had done, he might well have acted with impunity. But Shostakovich became a symphonist and operatic composer of international fame, who attracted the most serious attention. Even if he was considered to be a *yurodivy* – and Volkov states explicitly that this was the general view in his lifetime, not merely a later rationalisation – he exposed himself to enormous risk.

Thus far, Shostakovich's career had been crowned by success and official ap-proval. There were, however, profound changes afoot in his self-perception and creative persona, and Abraham very exactly identified their source. Immediately after finishing the Second Symphony, Shostakovich had begun work on an opera. If the symphonies had brought him academic recognition and official approval, he now seemed determined to produce a trickster work, frivolous, throwaway, double-wrapped in irony and impenetrable as to meaning and intention. At the simplest level, *The Nose* is a homage to a favourite writer. It is based on a short story by Nikolai Gogol who Shostakovich read avidly in his teens. The plot is scanty in the extreme. A bumptious Tsarist official, Kovalyov, wakens to find that his nose has gone off on its own and is enjoying the privileges and exerting some of the responsibilities of the Major's new office. There is a chase, and the nose is eventually restored to its proper position and function. Much pseudo-psychoana-lytic ink has been spilled in arguing a psycho-sexual interpretation of both story and opera. Such approaches work for Philip Roth's 1970s reworking *The Breast*, but they run aground on the deliberate thinness of Gogol's narrative, and Shosta-kovich's librettists' rather different version of it. What is important in both is the tone: dismissive, abrupt, more interested in the cadence of speech than in what is actually said. That there is less to *The Nose* than meets the eye is almost exactly what it is about.

At a personal level, the opera is influenced by the playful intelligence of Sollertinsky. It also derives something from the "biomechanical" theories of Vsevolod Meyerhold, with whom Shostakovich was working in Moscow in the spring of 1928. The immediate spark was seeing the first Russian production of Alban Berg's *Wozzeck* at the Mariinsky Theatre in Leningrad the previous year, a work which seemed to reflect something of Meyerhold's mechanistic approach to character. Some have suggested that the absurdist, anti-realistic tone of *The Nose* was in part influenced by Sergei Prokofiev's *Love for Three Oranges*, which had been premiered in Chicago in 1921, but received its first Russian performance also at the Mariinsky on February 18 1926, to enthusiastic acclaim. Shostakovich only met the older composer the following February, but there was a connection through Meyerhold, a supporter of both, who had adapted Carlo Gozzi's 18th century fairy tale, and used the same title, *Love for Three Oranges,* for his new journal devoted to study of *commedia dell'arte.* (The moonstruck protagonist of Arnold Schoenberg's *Pierrot Lunaire,* a work admired by Shostakovich, also derives from *commedia.*) The jester theme of *Oranges*, its clash between magic (dogma?) and laughter, and its premise in the Prince's chronic hypochondriasis seem to anticipate those of *The Nose* and Shostakovich's new-found *yurodivy* role, as does what Prokofiev's biographer Harlow Robinson characterises as the "aggressively stylized...and artificial" tone of the piece. The same words could be used of *The Nose*.

The work was given a concert performance in June 1929, amid considerable controversy, and then fully staged in January 1930, within twenty-four hours of the Third Symphony premiere. The opera's reception established a pattern: popular with the public, who flocked to more than a dozen performances at the Maly Opera in Leningrad; disliked by the musical watchdogs of RAPM, who objected to the work's lack of foundation in contemporary Soviet reality.

That reality was changing fast. Trotsky and Nikolai Bukharin were gone. The Soviet Union had entered into a period of enforced collectivisation and "superindustrialisation" under the first Five Year Plan. A cultural revolution that subordinated all expressive freedom and individuality to the needs of the Party was in progress. All art was to be proletarianised. A *Pravda* article by the country's new leader declared 1917 to be a cultural year zero. Mayakovsky offered the perfect metaphor for the creative artist's new situation when he took to playing Russian roulette. Shostakovich had his first serious taste of official disapproval, but had perhaps found a protective disguise as Pierrot, Harlequin and Fool.

Others were not so lucky. Vselovod Meyerhold was a prominent victim of the Soviet regime's about-face on experimentalism and the avant-garde. His work was declared to be alien to Soviet realities and the Meyerhold Theatre was closed in 1938. A year later, he was arrested and a "confession" obtained under torture. Meyerhold bravely withdrew it in court. He was executed by firing squad on February 1 or 2 1940. Ivan Sollertinsky's end was less dramatic, but the loss was no less grievous for Shostakovich. His friend – arguably his only real friend – succumbed to a heart attack at home in Novosibirsk, shortly before taking up a chair at the Moscow Conservatoire, a post which would have brought him closer to his old friend. In grief, Shostakovich wrote the Piano Trio No 2 in E minor, Op 67, one of his works which requires absolutely no effort of interpretation.

Finally, to Prokofiev. He had lived in Paris and worked abroad since 1920, but had been consistently admired at home. He visited Russia in 1927 and again in 1929, when his dissonant "industrial ballet" *Pas d'acier* was performed at Moscow's Beethoven Hall. A symphonic suite derived from the theatre work had been programmed in Moscow the previous year, to some acclaim, but admiration was more than usually fickle during the cultural revolution. RAPM condemned *Pas d'acier* as counter-revolutionary and hypothetically fascist. Prokofiev returned to Paris in a rage.

Shostakovich never seems to have contemplated exile, let alone defection, with any seriousness, and his inconsistent diatribes against Prokofiev and Stravinsky have much to do with their decision to live abroad. Prokofiev did, however, return to live in Russia from 1932 and his career and Shostakovich's run in intriguingly different directions for the next two decades. During the fraught and difficult mid-1930s, when Shostakovich wrestled with his problematic Fourth and Fifth Symphonies, Prokofiev seemed content to write songs and political cantatas, including one to mark the 20th anniversary of the Bolshevik Revolution, scored for choruses, military band, folksy accordions and percussion, and to texts by the great triumvirate of Soviet Communism. The work wasn't performed at the time, and was only heard in 1966, with one of the texts pointedly removed. Prokofiev lived on, internationally famous, trying to please the regime and criticised for it. His *Hymn to the Soviet Union* failed to win a wartime competition for a new national anthem; a song by Alexander Alexandrov, even more shamelessly patriotic, was chosen instead. As Harlow Robinson points out, "as Prokofiev's music was becoming more 'public', Shostakovich's was becoming more 'private'. While Prokofiev would write the explicitly nationalistic music for [Eisenstein's film] *Alexander Nevsky* in 1938, Shostakovich would write his First String Quartet." Prokofiev died, in his bed, on March 5 1953, the same day, as far as anyone can tell, as the man whose words would later be edited out of that celebratory cantata, the man who had ruled the Soviet Union for the past quarter century.

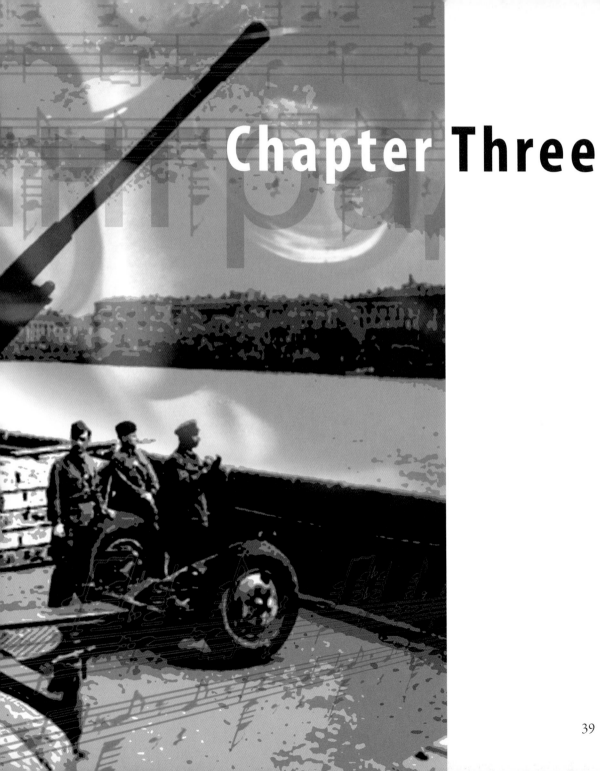

Chapter Three

Chapter Three

As a pianist, Shostakovich knew that the key to men's souls is not their eyes–his own shifted uneasily behind pebble-thick spectacles–but their hands. When he met Joseph Stalin, he saw before him "an ordinary, shabby little man, short, fat, with reddish hair. His face was covered with pockmarks and his right hand was noticeably thinner than his left. He kept hiding his right hand". There is a wealth of subtle malice in the description, which comes, inevitably, from *Testimony*, and just a tinge of "biomechanical" symbolism. Had that hand grown withered signing death warrants? Was it hidden out of guilt or guile?

Stalin ruled by intimidation. He is perhaps the greatest mass murderer of history, a dubious accolade which resists confirmation since no one will ever know how many died in cellars or in mass graves on his orders, or how many uncensused and illiterate peasants were systematically starved to death in accordance with his decrees. Hitler also hid a paretically tremulous hand behind his back, but Hitler did at least maintain some loyalties to the very end, and reserved some affection for friends and family members. Stalin spared no one; today's friend was tomorrow's inconvenience. Hitler may have put some squeamish distance between himself and the consequences of his edicts. Stalin did no such thing. The "Red Czar" overturned Nicholas I's famous comment that Russia was not ruled by him but by his 10,000 clerks. Stalin was what nowadays would be called a micromanager, and that extended to culture and the arts as well.

It is well known that Hitler's supposed passion for Wagner disguised a preference for light operetta. Most matters of high culture were left to the aesthete Goebbels. Stalin's real tastes were no more sophisticated and were largely satisfied by the little screening room in the Kremlin where the entire Politburo was often required to sit with him–or rather in the seats behind his private row–and watch either the latest release or an old favourite. According to Shostakovich, "Stalin loved films and he saw *The Great Waltz*, about Johann Strauss, many times, dozens of time. He also liked Tarzan films". Johnny Weissmuller notwithstanding, Stalin considered himself a man of taste and discrimination and amply qualified to meddle in the music of a man like Dmitri Shostakovich.

They make a curious pair, the dictator and the composer, but for the next twenty years J V Stalin and D D Shostakovich were to observe the steps of a strange and very Russian dance, its choreography an amalgam of ideology and principle, its metre irregular, its course along the edge of a precipice. Shostakovich may have hinted at his presence in the clanking cadences of the Second Symphony. He later – in 1957 and still secretly – adapted Mussorgsky's *Rayok* as a skit on the former regime, with Stalin cast as "Edinitsyn", which means "number one", but also "the dunce". It's a sign that, however "harsh and intolerant" he may have seemed (and that is his own description of his younger self) Shostakovich had a sense of humour, a great sense of fun and was by all accounts a fiendish poker player.

It is important to distinguish between the stressed and undernourished man who visited America after the Second World War and the 24 year old who had recovered from most of his childhood and teenage ills and was being bruited about as the coming man in Russian, or Soviet, music. Isaak Glikman, who became Shostakovich's friend and secretary in the 1930s described him as looking younger than his years. "I was captivated by the refinement of his face, its individuality, its noble aspect...In many early descriptions, Shostakovich is depicted as physically weak, frail, and even puny but these are extremely misleading statements. In my view, Shostakovich was of decent height, slender, yet supple and strong. His clothes always suited him...His head was crowned with wonderful dark, copper-coloured hair, which was carefully combed, or else fell in poetic disorder". Here is a description to set alongside Shostakovich's thumbnail sketch of Stalin! The key word in it is "captivated". Even those who sensed a troubled soul behind the wise, grey eyes, or who saw the floppy fringe as part of his camouflage were instinctively impressed. This was the forceful young man who married Nina Varzar in May 1932 and forged a relationship so strong for all its volatility that the couple remarried immediately after their divorce in the spring of 1935, and started a family: Galina a year later, and the future conductor Maxim two years after that.

To hear Shostakovich's music as uniformly dark and tragic, without an appreciation of its moments of comedy, black or lighter, distorts it every bit as much as to consider it monolithically "pro-Soviet" or "anti-Communist". His insistence that *The Nose* should be heard as a horror story rather than a comedy was, of course, partly tongue-in-cheek, the *yurodivy* concealing his real meaning. Between the work's concert and stage premieres, the country had just celebrated Stalin's 50th birthday, the beginnings of the "cult of the personality" later denounced by Nikita Khrushchev. Few of its audience could have missed the humour or the horror of Gogol's parable, or indeed who Shostakovich intended in that runaway organ.

So far, at least, he was not suspected of anti-Soviet, or indeed anti-Stalin expression. Indeed, so much was Shostakovich the coming man that he was inundated with commissions, many of them infinitely more absurd in conception than *The Nose*. Shostakovich was an avid soccer fan – a photograph from the 1940s finds him at a match with friends, shouting lustily at the camera – and a natural choice to write the music for what was intended to be an appropriately modern and appropriately Soviet ballet, something that might preserve Russian pre-eminence in the dance but ease out the tired old bourgeois repertoire on which that reputation had been founded. Originally called *Dynamaida*, the libretto told the utterly unsurprising story of a Soviet team's heroic triumph over a pack of bourgeois-fascist hackers and cheats. As *The Golden Age* it was, Shostakovich said, a "chilly success" and was quietly, in footballing parlance, sidelined.

There were other commissions as well. Shostakovich reacted caustically to the libretto provided for another ballet, originally to be called *The New Machine*. Sarcasm drips off every line of a letter to Sollertinsky. "The theme is extremely relevant. There once was a machine. Then it broke down (problem of material decay). Then it was mended (problem of amortization) and at the same time they bought a new one. Then everybody dances around the new machine. Apotheosis. This all takes up three acts". *The Bolt,* as it was eventually called, was quickly shot, though perversely Shostakovich was blamed in some quarters for its failure. It had been intended to serve as an allegorical warning to industrial "wreckers", 53 of whom from Donbass had been subjected to one of the first Stalinist show trials in the summer of 1928.

A more agreeable subject presented itself at the end of 1931. That Shostakovich should in later years have been identified with the morose, introspective, procrastinating Prince of Denmark is doubly ironic given the "revisionist" nature of Nikolai Akimov's production. The director reasoned that in the fast-moving and forward-looking Soviet Union no-one would want to watch some decadent royal agonising over philosophical issues. His solution: fill the stage with sword-play, hunts and battle scenes; create a spectacular banquet; make the victorious Fortinbras the dramatic heart of the piece. Shostakovich used jazz elements in his score, notably when a drunken Ophelia sings a cabaret song, but he also took the opportunity to poke fun at "official" Soviet composers when in one notorious scene, obviously worked out between director and composer, Hamlet farts through a flute - some remember it being posed jutting from his groin like an erect penis – while the piccolo in the pit orchestra plays an out-of-tune version of a recent "hit" by Alexander Davidenko written to celebrate Soviet victories on the Chinese border.

There was, of course, somewhat more to Akimov's *Hamlet* than a Hollywood-styled confection. The Prince was portrayed as a kind of revolutionary, battling the decadence of the court, but also as an ambitious fraud, cooking up the story of his father's ghost to ease his own path to the throne. The production, which opened at the Vakhtangov Theatre just a few days before Shostakovich's wedding, was a *succès de scandale.* Official protests failed to dent its popularity, nor did it seem to weaken Shostakovich's position. Akimov, too, seemed for the moment untouchable, though his days were clearly numbered. For the moment, and particularly with the suppression of the ACM, music wasn't the main object of government strictures. It was literature, a far more obvious source of subversion, which exercised the authorities. Mayakovsky had been hounded to death, Osip Mandelstam, whose *Kamen* (1913), *Tristia* (1922) and *Stikhotvoreniya* (1928) had established him as the greatest Russian poet of the century, was banished from Leningrad. A decade after his last book was published, he died on his way to a labour camp; a heart attack cheated the authorities of their revenge. Yevgeny Zamyatin, whose *We* (1920) had predicted the rise of Stalin, asked to go into exile. He was refused but on the intercession of Maxim Gorky, the regime relented and Zamyatin eventually died in Paris. Gorky had taken

Shostakovich held his children, Galina and Maxim, in great affection. Was it something in the story that amused them?

the opposite route. The author of *The Lower Depths* (1902) and a brilliant autobiographical trilogy had been in London with Lenin, which lent him a certain revolutionary allure. He had lived abroad for long periods, partly for his health, partly as an inveterate nomad, but had always returned home when his country needed him, as in 1914 and again in 1928, when he became the iconic Soviet writer, a staunch defender of what became known as "Socialist Realism".

This, for the moment, was the cultural battleground, but it would not be long before Shostakovich came under scrutiny. His next major project would also have a (loosely) Shakespearean association and it would be the most remarkable but also the most problematic work of his career so far. For the moment, though, he had found in *Hamlet* and in the figure of the Prince a model for his own creative behaviour: disguising his deeper, slower evolution behind a facade of accommodating activity, all the time refusing to be a pipe that others could play on, farting inaudibly under cover of the noise and brouhaha and then denying that the bad smell was his. A worse odour was to follow, though, and with dangerous consequences.

It is perhaps the most famous bad review in musical history. It is also not quite clearly understood. On January 28 1936, Shostakovich was in Arkhangel, the latest stop on a tour round Russia. A draft of the Fourth Symphony was in his briefcase. What he read in that morning's edition of *Pravda* would in due course lead to the shelving of the symphony, but must at the time have made the 30 year old composer's blood run cold. The headline ran "Muddle Instead of Music". The opera so described was condemned as a "leftist bedlam" and "petty bourgeois clowning". The composer "apparently does not set himself the task of listening to the desires and expectations of the Soviet public. He scrambles sounds to make them interesting to formalist elements who have lost all taste". The piece also contained what could only have been construed as a threat: "This game may end badly".

What made the article doubly chilling was that it was unsigned. That usually meant that it had been written by Stalin himself, though in this case it seems to have been written by a functionary – or tame journalist – called David Zaslavsky. To compound the irony, Shostakovich had written part of the score while once again in holiday in Georgia, but this time in Tbilisi, Stalin's place of birth. He had been much interrupted, not least by the need to fulfil commissions for TRAM and other official companies. He had written *Rule Britannia,* music for film, and a strange revue called *Allegedly Murdered*. He had, though, pulled out of theatre work and embarked on a new symphony to be called *From Karl Marx To Our Own Days*. It was later abandoned. Eventually, in December 1932, he finished his opera. During the inevitable delay before its first production, Shostakovich completed other works. His Twenty-Four Preludes for piano were written, seemingly, as daily exercises. If they do represent a kind of musical diary, they offer a disturbing view of the composer's frame of mind at the time. Though written as an orthodox Bachian "cycle of fifths", they are brief, bitter and throwaway, and as sarcastic as Prokofiev. So was the Op 35 Piano Concerto No 1 in C minor written at the same time, where Shostakovich follows the older composer's example in cocking a snook at the Romantic concertos of Tchaikovsky and Rachmaninov, with their implicitly "confessional" manner. As it progresses, though, the work does go deeper, and seems to imply a continuity between the expressive extremes of Romanticism and the libertinism of the revolutionary years, and then between that hectic modernity and the intellectual calm and simplicity of purpose of Bach and Haydn. In its jazzy rhythms, curiously detached viewpoint, and sour opposition of past and present, it has something in common with T S Eliot's *The Waste Land*, and is a similar triumph of ventriloquism.

There is a persistent misconception that Shostakovich's *Lady Macbeth of Mtsensk,* now regarded as one of the great operas of the 20th century, was a failure and a critical disaster, and that the "Muddle" review in *Pravda* followed its first performances. To the contrary, the piece was Shostakovich's next great triumph after the First Symphony. It was premiered simultaneously in Moscow and Leningrad in January 1934 and was rapturously received. The piece ran for nearly two years and its success gave Shostakovich and Nina a measure of domestic security; when they parted briefly in the summer of 1934, economic issues may have played a part – Nina came, after all, from a properous family – and better prospects must have played some part in their reconciliation.

All seemed well with Shostakovich and his opera until Stalin attended a performance at the Bolshoi in the first weeks of 1936, and apparently reached the paranoid (but not necessarily inaccurate) conclusion that the character of the police chief in the third act was a skit on himself. These scenes were not in the original story, which gives the possibility some added credence. Shostakovitch had turned to a short novel published in 1865 by Nikolai Leskov, in which he saw a powerful allegory of life in pre-Revolutionary Russia and a possible first part of what he optimistically conceived as a Wagnerian cycle that would look at the heroic role of women in the liberation of his country. (His *narodnik* background would have come out in a second opera, about the People's Will revolutionary Sofia Perovskaya, who had organised the assassination of Alexander II; it was never written.)

It is hard, at first glance, to detect the heroic strain in its heroine Katerina Ismailova, whose name was used for Soviet productions and in the West for Shostakovich's later, bowdlerised version; outside Russia, the opera is usually known by the title of Leskov's story. The main difference between the original text and Shostakovich's and librettist Alexander Preis's version is the relative sympathy accorded the heroine, which is why the Russian change of title makes sense. Katerina is trapped in a loveless marriage to a country merchant, Zinovy Ismailovich, and bullied by her father-in-law Boris Timofeevich, whose arrival is heralded by a pompous bassoon melody. In the opening scene, he attacks her for having failed to produce an heir, accuses her of contemplating infidelity, and then, unwisely, reminds her to set out poison for the rats that are gnawing away at their stock.

Zinovy appears to announce that he must go and mend a broken dam – dam-building and the fear of sabotage were powerful signifiers in Soviet Russia – and introduces a new servant, Sergei, who has apparently been dismissed from a previous job for seducing his mistress. Boris demands that Katerina swear an oath of fidelity. So far, the piece has a cheerfully Mozartian contrivance and air of inevitability. There are, however, already signs of cruelty. The servants, who have sarcastically fawned over their master, begging him not to go (dissent by exaggeration?), now torture Aksinya, one of their number, as if she were a pig fattened for market. Katerina breaks them up, but finds herself grappling with Sergei, which is seen by her father-in-law. Already she seems sensitive, considerate, a flower in the desert rather than an ambitious Lady Macbeth, bored rather than wicked. That is confirmed in the next scene when she appears at her window and sings with unbearable loneliness "Zherebyonok k kobylke toropitsa" ("the colt runs after the filly"), comparing her own lot to that of the animals and the birds who are governed by more natural instincts.

On the pretext of borrowing a book, Sergei seduces her. Boris prowls about below, boasting of his own youthful prowess and clearly considering the possibility of bedding his daughter-in-law when he discovers that the manservant has beaten him to it. His lust is channelled into sadism as he flogs Sergei. Tired but satisfied, he demands supper. The mushrooms are poisoned. Boris dies just as the priest arrives, accusing Katerina of murder.

The scene ends with the priest wittering about the difference between a man's death and a rat's and quoting Gogol on the perils of mushrooms and cold soups. What follows is the most extraordinary moment in the opera, a huge entr'acte in the form of a passacaglia, signalled by discordant blasts of brass. It arguably represents the most effective orchestral writing yet from Shostakovich, summing up the looming tragedy of the opening scenes.

Sergei turns out to be more potent than Zinovy but without much stamina or spiritual substance behind his "educated" exterior. As the huge passacaglia ebbs away, Katerina wants to make love, but her "Seryozha" merely wants to sleep. They are briefly haunted by Boris's ghost, but it turns out to be the returning Zinovy, who is murdered in turn. Accompanied by one of Shostakovich's grotesque marches, they bury the body in the cellar, the mood darkening with every measure.

On the lovers' wedding day a drunk man decides to raid the cellar for more booze and the body is discovered, stinking of decay. The police, irritated that they have not been invited to the celebrations and bored with questioning a hapless nihilist, are galvanised by news of the body's discovery. Katerina and Sergei are arrested and condemned to exile. In one of Shostakovich's extraordinary changes of face, the mood turns from farcical to tragic at the beginning of Act IV. An old prisoner sings of the long road to Siberian exile in tones that irresistibly recall Mussorgsky. Katerina bribes a pass into the men's part of the prison but is cruelly rejected by her husband; this inspires a beautiful little *arioso* lament acccompanied by cor anglais.

Sergei has begun to flirt with another convict Sonyetka and persuades Katerina to give up her stockings as a gift to the latest object of his affections. Katerina weeps herself to sleep and is roused by the old convict just as the sergeant organises the prisoners' column for the long walk to Siberia. Spotting Sonyetka standing on a bridge, Katerina grabs her and the two women plunge into the fast-flowing waters below.

A plot that involved two murders, promiscuity, and a murder-suicide: this was not necessarily the stuff of "affirmative" Soviet opera. It did, however, strike deep chords with its audience, who would not have missed the vicious satire directed at the old regime and might very well have appreciated Shostakovich's instinctive feminism. He is clearly sympathetic to Katerina and her plight– her lament reappeared at a key moment in his highly personal Eighth Quartet for strings – and seems to have treated her murders as legitimate killings. There were, however, other strands to the opera, working at ever deeper levels, not least a palpable nostalgia for the old Russia and its musics (some of the convict songs were a legacy from his mother, who remembered them from her journeys in Siberia) and by extension its gentler sexual politics.

Shostakovich was drawn to Leskov as one of the few convincing heirs of Gogol (hence the reference), and an important transitional figure for writers of the Zamyatin generation. *Lady Macbeth of Mtsensk* is an infinitely subtler and grander work than *The Nose*, but its targets and its obsessions are essentially the same, and its tone essentially tragic. That may have appealed to opera goers, but it did not square with official thinking. The word "Formalist" in that *Pravda* review was a hand grenade thrown into Shostakovich's lap. It wasn't the first time that it had been used. The previous February the other important daily journal had complained of formalist elements in the opera, but an article in *Izvestia* did not have the same official force as an unsigned leader in *Pravda*, which is why Shostakovich responded forcefully to the first accusation, but largely kept his own counsel over the second. There were other factors, too.

In the same month as *Lady Macbeth of Mtsensk* was premiered, Stalin announced to the 17th Party Congress, the "Congress of Victors", that socialism had been achieved. The price of victory was horrific. The first Five Year Plan had ended some twenty months previously and left the country exhausted. Political purges had liquidated some one million individuals. The Russian countryside was effectively locked down; eight million, and probably more, died as a result of collectivisation. In the summer of 1934 Stalin re-organised and renamed his secret police, OGPU became NKVD. On the first day of December, his last remaining rival, the hugely popular Sergei Kirov was shot dead in Leningrad. Though Stalin himself or someone close to him had undoubtedly sent the young gunman Leonid Nikolayev, the new police force was able to find some 40,000 "fellow-conspirators" and send them off to the camps.

This was victory indeed, and it fell to writers and composers to reflect the "joyfulness" of Soviet life in their work. Optimism was compulsory; pessimism outlawed. Any sense of art as evolutionary struggle was suspended in light of Soviet victory and the triumphant Communist synthesis. The proletarian organisations which had overseen creative endeavour were disbanded and centralised; the Politburo, or more probably Stalin himself, was the only arbiter of taste. Irony and tragedy, self-conscious modernity, self-serving experiment, were all lumped together under a term that surfaced (to Shostakovich's fury) in that *Pravda* editorial. If in "Socialist Realism" Stalin had found a useful shorthand for all that was good and positive in Soviet art, in the same way "Formalism" and "Formalist" did service for anything non-approved, from painterly abstraction to reactionary nostalgia in either music or print. The distinction was full of logical contradictions, probably better understood in Russia than in the West, but it was never intended to be anything other than a highly adaptable blunt instrument. Novelists were called on to churn out huge affirmative narratives whose only rationale was to underline the viciousness of the *ancién regime,* the triumph of Bolshevism, and by extension the unassailable goodness and wisdom of the *Vozhd,* or Leader. Painters and sculptors no longer had to search for subjects: avoid mere pattern-making; celebrate the heroic endeavours of the Soviet worker and soldier, and their sturdy, beautiful helpmeets and children; avoid private gestures; work on the largest scale; understand that Stalin himself was an icon of victory and progress.

Things weren't quite as simple for composers of music. Some key signatures and modes were understood to be "counter-revolutionary". Minor keys perhaps suggested defeatism. Too much slow music might suggest that all was not well with the Soviet apotheosis after all. Western importations were simply a new form of "intervention". To some degree, all instrumental music is formalist, autotelic. Unless one imitates natural sounds – birdsong, or the factory hooters Shostakovich brings into the Second Symphony – orchestral and chamber music can have no absolute meaning, or at least none beyond what the composer, his listeners and his critics choose to impose on it. There is a simple enough solution, one Shostakovich had already tried. Just as artists were encouraged to add appropriate texts where there was any remote possibility of ambiguity, so composers were enjoined to add appropriate titles to their works and to construct song-symphonies that removed all need to interpret the music. All one needed to do was listen to the words.

Whatever Shostakovich meant by his Second and Third Symphonies, he had become a master of ambiguity. The text of *Lady Macbeth of Mtsensk* is subtly inflected,

Ivan Sollertinsky was the most important friend of Shostakovich's lifetime, his premature death caused him the deepest grief

but so too is its score. By contrast his ballet *The Limpid Stream,* which followed and enjoyed a milder but comparable success, is the blandest propaganda. The paradox only troubles if both works are lifted out of context. What better response to the suggestion that you are "Formalist" than to write a work of numbing orthodoxy? Why then was the ballet criticised alongside the opera in the pages of *Pravda*?

The simple answer was that Shostakovich himself had become suspect, even if individual works were not. In February 1936, he was even deserted by friends and colleagues, when the Leningrad and Moscow Composers' Union voted unanimously in support of the *Pravda* article. Among those who ratified its findings was his "idolator" Ivan Sollertinsky, though Shostakovich probably gave the decision his blessing, rather than expose his friend to isolation and possible harm. Another friend, the brilliant critic Boris Asafiev declared that his own initial enthusiasm had been in error and that the true direction of Soviet opera was to be found in Ivan

ДМИТРИЙ ДМИТРИЕВИЧ ШОСТАКОВИЧ

Dzerzhinsky's *The Quiet Don,* adapted from Mikhail Sholokhov's novel *Quiet Flows the Don*, and dedicated to Shostakovich ironically. Asafiev also reversed his judgement of *The Limpid Stream*; now *it* was the major work and *Lady Macbeth* the formalist farrago. What part professional jealousy played in all this can only be guessed at, but it left Shostakovich, for all his fame, dangerously isolated.

He would have recognised, especially after *The Limpid Stream,* that one potential tactic was silence. There was the example of Boris Pasternak, who had stopped writing in 1933, rather than write puffs for the regime and rather than risk liquidation by openly criticising it. There was also the option of exile. For every artist that had come home to support the Revolution, there were others who had left or who, like Stravinsky, ostentatiously stayed away. Maxim Gorky had returned to give some theoretical mass to the idea of "Socialist Realism"; Zamyatin was in Paris. Shostakovich seemed to prefer a kind of self-imposed internal exile, not the banishment handed out to Pasternak for a more unguarded moment a little later, but a certain distance and removal.

Shostakovich had largely stayed out of the debates on Soviet symphonism held at the Composers' Union the previous February, doubtless already thinking about his own Fourth (and if Glikman is to be believed, his Fifth as well). Nor did he at first see fit to change his position on *Lady Macbeth of Mtsensk,* opting neither to defend the work further nor to disown it (though he told one friend that in the unlikely event of the latter happening, it would be 100%). More important, he was not on this occasion required to recant publicly, as he would be a dozen years later. The "untiring troubadour of Leftist distortion" (as *Pravda* called him) apologised quietly for his errors to his colleagues at the Composers' Union. Nor did he disappear, like a million others, or countless others still to come. Stalin seemed to have other plans for Shostakovich and they were crueller for being more playful. If there is a Fool, there has to be a King and it may be that Stalin took on the role with every bit as much ironic awareness as the man who had once been tipped to become his court composer. Shostakovich's works were banned from performance and publication, but he was not completely silenced. The Fourth Symphony, finished a matter of days before the birth of his daughter Galya in May 1937, was put into rehearsal with the Leningrad Philharmonic, and only withdrawn when the composer finally lost patience with conductor Fritz Stiedry, who seemed to be making a botch of things. He was not a poor musician and so must have been in an agony of doubt and anxiety, his hand too shaky to sustain the symphony's pounding metres. Rehearsal of a chamber piece could have been kept secret, but not a work requiring orchestral forces. So were the authorities tacitly rehabilitating Shostakovich? Or had the axe simply not yet fallen? Or was the whole thing part of some larger, capricious game? The Kirov assassination had changed the rules dramatically, and instilled a deep paranoia. Even some of those not arrested as "conspirators" committed suicide before they heard the knock on the door, and Shostakovich himself seems to have considered ending his own life. Deep down he knew that the smell of death wasn't going to be limited to the Ismailov's cellar. Over the next three years, it would pervade every government cellar and official basement, and would seep into the unconscious of every thinking Russian.

Chapter Four

Муза-сестра заглянула в ли[цо,]
Взгляд ее ясен и ярок.
И отняла золотое кольцо,
Первый весенний подаро[к.]
Муза! ты видишь, как счастлив[ы все —]
Девушки, женщины, вдов[ы...]
Лучше погибну на колесе[,]
Только не эти оковы.
Знаю: гадая, и мне обрыва[ть]
Нежный цветок маргаритк[и.]
Должен на этой земле испы[тать]
Каждый любовную пытк[у.]
Жгу до зари на окошке све[чу]
И ни о ком не тоскую,
Но не хочу, не хочу, не хоч[у]
Знать, как целуют другую[.]
Завтра мне скажут, смеясь, зер[кала:]
"Взор твой не ясен, не яро[к..."]
Тихо отвечу: "Она отняла
Божий подарок".

Chapter Four

If "Muddle Instead of Music" is one of the most notorious music reviews ever published, the eventual reply is equally infamous. What it means has been debated for 70 years and adduced in evidence for diametrically opposite conclusions. On November 21 1937 at the Philharmonic Hall in Leningrad, Shostakovich unveiled his Symphony No 5 in D minor, Op 47. The score bore the inscription "Practical creative reply of a Soviet musician to just criticism". The adjectives are worth considering. Did Shostakovich now accept that the humiliation of February 1936 had really been "just"? Had he now fallen into line as a "Soviet" composer, alert to the needs of Socialist Realism and the almost papal infallibility of the *Vozhd*? Or was there a sleight-of-hand in the use of "creative"? Was this seeming recantation merely red-coloured smoke to throw off the watching apparatchiks? There is a further question, and by no means an absurd one given Shostakovich's willingness to sign statements he had not written: were the words his at all?

The previous spring Shostakovich had become a non-person. His music was not being played publicly and given the paranoia of a society in which a young boy –Pavlik Morozov – could be declared a national hero for betraying his own father to the authorities it was unlikely to be played privately either. Old friends and associates crossed the street to avoid him. Shostakovich seems to have drifted into a suicidal lethargy, relieved only partially by a visit to his influential friend and former patron Mikhail Tukhachevsky, a senior Marshal in the Soviet Army and a music lover who had access to Stalin. Even though Tukhachevsky seems to have reassured him that the feared midnight knock on the door was not imminent (that fate ultimately awaited the Marshal himself), Shostakovich was chronically anxious and utterly alienated.

In that he was not alone. More than one observer has described the average Soviet citizen's life during the Great Terror as a species of universal solitary confinement. If a child could betray his father, and friends could publicly condemn a once-admired colleague, there were no limits to fear; this is what is meant by totalitarianism. In Shostakovich's case the visit to Tukhachevsky did at least allow him to start writing music again, playing and improvising with some renewed vigour. Small wonder, though, that the work he produced should itself have been totalising and excessive.

The Fourth Symphony is both a portrait of Shostakovich at his lowest ebb, haunted by a motif that seems to communicate betrayal, and also a portrait of a country where every ordinary cultural parameter seemed cubistically distorted. The summer of 1936 saw more show-trials. Having eliminated the old Bolsheviks, Stalin now set about getting rid of the "United Centre". The head of the NKVD was arrested for falling behind schedule in uncovering counter-revolutionary plots. Half a million were reportedly shot, millions more deported to Siberia and likely death. The heros of the hour were the "shockworkers" of the second Five Year Plan. The first and most famous of them all was Aleksei Grigorievich Stakhanov, who on August 31 1935 mined 102 tons of coal in a single, six-hour shift, fourteen times his quota. Others quickly followed, Alexander Busygin in the automobile industry, Maria Vinogradov in textiles, Maria Demchenko in agriculture, and the Stakhanov movement was born. It was, of course, all carefully stage-managed, the flipside of *vranyo* exaggeration-as-satire, and was a defining aspect of the obsessive gigantomania that some observers have seen as characteristic of Soviet life at the time, and which Shostakovich "self-critically" noted in the finale to his withdrawn Fourth Symphony.

His precarious standing with the authorities apart, he had every good reason to have high hopes of the work. The night before Galina was born, Shostakovich and Nina entertained the conductor Otto Klemperer, a great champion of his work in the West who had regularly programmed the First Symphony, along with the First Piano Concerto and the ballet suites from *The Golden Age* and *The Bolt*. A play-through of the new score was arranged on two pianos and Klemperer was again much impressed. It became a double celebration when Nina gave birth. However, things were proceeding disastrously with rehearsals and, apparently on the recommendation of Philharmonic director I M Renzin, Shostakovich agreed to cancel the performance. Dangerous rumours had already circulated that the symphony was ridden with "Formalism". Renzin would not have relished any possibility of guilt-by-association.

The score was lost during the war and subsequently reconstructed from a two-piano version. Twenty-five years after its abandonment, and two months after the premiere of the Twelfth Symphony before the 22nd Congress of the Soviet Communist Party, the Fourth was performed in Moscow. It is immediately and strikingly different from its predecessors. Where they tended to begin quietly and with consideration, the Fourth opens *fortissimo*, establishing the blaring intensity it maintains almost all the way through. There is a calculated crudity to some of the figuration, reminiscent of parts of *Lady Macbeth of Mtsensk* and particularly of the priest's music and the police scenes. There is a quieter passage for strings in the opening movement, which without overt quotation nevertheless manages to hint at classical models, but tattered and almost off-hand, ripped fragments of old scores eddying about in the Soviet whirlwind, almost silenced and lost in Shostakovich's overwrought memory. He had done something similar in the Cello Sonata in D minor, Op 40, finished exactly a year before he began work on the symphony in September 1935.

The movement oscillates uneasily– as the composer's life and work would – between vast declamatory climaxes and a kind of night-music, in which muttered ideas and memories are anxiously self-censored. A bassoon theme, punctuated by harp-chimes, seems to conjure up insomnia. The loud subjects will not go away, however, and just as there seems to be a promise of dawn and humane company, there is a fresh irruption that some hear as the arrival of the long-feared secret police. It is an exhausting and determinedly ugly movement. Whatever its programmatic meaning, there is no mistaking its technical novelty and boldness. Significantly, Christopher Ballantine devotes more space to it in his *Twentieth Century Symphony* (1983) than to any other Shostakovich work. In a chapter headed "Radical Structural Innovation" he lays out the opening movement's tonal ambiguities, its avoidance of classical development and its parodic elements (like the sour waltz in C# minor that precedes the complex recapitulation.) "I am not afraid of difficulties", Shostakovich is supposed to have said during the writing of the Fourth. Whether he meant his present parlous political state or the structural challenges of the new symphony isn't clear, but both can reasonably be assumed. If the Fourth Symphony is thematically disturbing, as a naturalistic portrait of the composer's surroundings and state of mind, it is even more alien in terms of symphonic language. Even so, underneath its roiling surface, there is still something of the language of Haydn and Beethoven, fragmented and embattled but imparting a precarious centripetal gravity to the piece.

The second movement is more explicitly traditional, relying on a Beethoven-like four-note figure and a relatively clear alternation of subjects. It ends, however, with a further echo of the first movement's Valley of Dry Bones, a quietly hellish vision that for all its deceptive calm fails to reassure. The closing movement is as disturbing as the first and even louder. There is a bleak funeral march, reminiscent of Mahler. There is, though, no time for mourning. The interment seems to be taking place in the middle of an earthquake. The mourners, if such they be, laugh caustically. Shostakovich briefly seems to lament his loss: hopes, friends, memories, not so much dead and lost as denied and disappeared. The march steadily mounts up to a climax of impossible force, arguably the loudest music ever written for a conventional orchestra.

Ian MacDonald describes the Fourth as a "milestone in symphonism". At the time, it was a millstone. Had the work been performed as planned in 1936, it might have proved the final straw and D D Shostakovich might well have joined the long line of the disappeared. On the other hand, its appearance then might have emboldened other symphonic composers in Russia and the West to experiment more dangerously with the form. When it was eventually played, it seemed both a problematic period-piece, coloured by what had happened to Shostakovich and to the Soviet Union in the intervening years, and somehow ripped out of context. It was certainly heard with anachronistic ears in the West, with little understanding of the circumstances behind it.

And yet, how different in tone, manner and intention is the Fourth from its successor? The Fifth Symphony, like the Cello Sonata as well, is another minor key work, no less deceptive in mocking, its acceptance by the regime a symptom of wishful thinking on the grandest scale.

The Terror continued. Stalin consistently portrayed the Revolution as beset by wreckers and counter-revolutionaries on all sides. As the second Five Year Plan came to an end in April 1937, arrests of army and government officials intensified; even Tukhachevsky fell victim, which must have given Shostakovich renewed anxiety. There were more show-trials, again directed at largely imaginary cabals. The "Right-Trotskyites" included such unlikely bedfellows as former NKVD chief Yagoda (accused of running his labour camps

Looking more that usually strained Shostakovich is photographed in Prague with conductor Evgeny Mravinsky and violinist David Oistrakh.

like spas) and the brilliant Nikolai Bukharin, one of the finest Bolshevik minds. The death toll becomes increasingly abstract as numbers mount through the millions.

Shostakovich, though, must have had some modest ground for hope. He continued to work on film and theatre projects and in the spring of 1937 was asked to give composition and orchestration classes at Leningrad Conservatory. A year in purdah may have been deemed sufficient for the moment. A full-scale rehabilitation still seemed some way off. Working at his alma mater also afforded time for work of his own, rather than official commissions. Between April and July, Shostakovich worked on the score of his Fifth – and ultimately most celebrated – Symphony.

Though he continued to produce music for cinema, Shostakovich only wrote one other significant score in 1937. The *Four Pushkin Romances* revived a literary passion of the composer's teenage years. The work carries opus number 46, immediately before that of the Fifth Symphony in his catalogue of works and the two works have a buried connection. Though the *Romances* were not heard until 1940, Shostakovich used the opening phrase from his setting for one of the poems, significantly called "Rebirth" as the basis of the great march theme in the symphony. Such self-quotation, common enough among very prolific composers, became an obsession with Shostakovich. What is important here is the text that the phrase introduced. "So, delusion falls away from my tormented soul, and reveals to me a vision of my former innocence".

The official Soviet line on the Fifth Symphony was that it represented an artist who had recognised the limitations of individualism and the redundancy of tragedy as a philosophical position and had succeeded through struggle in re-aligning himself with the masses. Whether that was the illusion that Shostakovich felt dropping away or whether he had simply discovered a way of retaining his innocence – "purity" might be a more accurate translation – underneath a carapace of conformity remains the issue. One stock metaphor cast Shostakovich once again as Hamlet, but a Hamlet who had risen above metaphysical dithering to claim his place in the world. So comfortable a critical shorthand was this that some Russians even today refer to the Fifth as "the Hamlet Symphony". Beware the pitfalls of metaphor, though. Perhaps this fallen prince of Russian music was still mad and dissembling sanity...

Shostakovich's Symphony No 5 in D minor, Op 47 was performed at Leningrad's Philharmonic Hall on November 21 1937. The conductor was Evgeny Mravinsky, who along with Kyrill Kondrashin, was Shostakovich's favourite. The atmosphere was electric. Though the audience could not have known it, what they heard in the opening movement was a radical simplification of the dense, textural language of the withdrawn Fourth. Having been damned for "Formalist" complexity, Shostakovich set out from the beginning to demonstrate that he could write with apparent simplicity. Some argue that his model for this was Gustav Mahler's Fourth Symphony, which disguises its darker significance behind a child-like exterior.

Much of the opening movement is built from a two-note motto, reminiscent of some of the music in *Lady Macbeth of Mtsensk* but a common device throughout Shostakovich's output to date. The difference here is that what was usually accompaniment is now promoted to main structural device. Like an architect previously criticised for excessive decoration and non-functional ideas, Shostakovich is working with concrete and iron braces. The movement takes on an aspect that resembles Beethoven's Symphony No 6 "Pastoral", where the bucolic landscape is threatened by an encroaching storm. Here, though, the threat is not lightning and rain but whatever is represented by the stomping of brass and low percussion that seem to cut through the music. If this is really meant to represent Stalin and his gang, Shostakovich was being suicidally brave. The change of atmosphere is palpable. Something has altered radically, and not for the better. The tonal material is soured and rhythmically uncertain. The two-note figure now finds itself in awkward contexts. A pall of fear settles across the remainder of the movement.

The Scherzo is precisely that, a broad joke that raises the banality of the first movement into a general principle. Here, it says, is the world in which we now live, all forced merriment and unthinking certainty; they lead, we follow; they say "Jump!", we ask "How high?" One instrument or instrumental group follows another, often required to play outside normal range or character. There is no real question-and-answer, merely an awkward consensus learned by rote.

Shostakovich had made his reputation with the First Symphony and here again he makes the same dramatic transition from farce to tragedy, from mere cleverness to deeper feelings. However, where the last two movements of the First were pastiche, the remainder of the Fifth was all his own. The Largo is unbearably intense and much of the audience on November 21 1937 was in tears as it unfolded, thirteen minutes of unmistakable evocation. On June 13, Tukhachevsky had been shot, accused of plotting with Hitler to overthrow the *Vozhd*. Shostakovich's slow movement is a memorial to his friend, but also to every other Russian marched away at midnight – the music is utterly nocturnal – to a muffled execution.

At this point in the First, Shostakovich simply intensified the tragic sense. Circumstances had radically changed, though. Something very different was called for here. The finale plunges back into the unnatural daylight, the tremulous quality of the slow movement transformed into "affirmation". As ever, Shostakovich's structural control and ability to integrate multiple frequencies and apparently unrelated components is uncanny. All the scattered elements of the first movement and scherzo are drawn back in to some of the densest writing of his career. Not even the clashing sound-masses of the Fourth approach this level of synthesis. And yet the tone is unremittingly ironic. It is as if Shostakovich is saying: You demand an apotheosis? *Here* is your apotheosis! And throws it down defiantly. (He makes clear in *Testimony* that any affirmation to be found in the closing movement is of the hollowest sort.)

As this strange, disturbing music played out, members of the audience in the Philharmonic Hall rose to their feet one by one. The ovation lasted longer than the symphony itself. Mravinksy, who had had problems with Shostakovich over the correct tempi and had resorted to subterfuge to force the composer to make his intentions plain, turned at the podium and raised the score high over his head, as if to say that it was the work and not the performance that should be applauded. Similar scenes played out at the first performance in Moscow the following January, and at a subsequent performance in Leningrad a group of Party officials climbed onto the platform and proposed that a telegram of congratulation be sent to Shostakovich from the whole audience.

The non-person had become the People's Artist. Shostakovich's rehabilitation seemed as mystifyingly complete as it was sudden. The Fifth Symphony became the core of the Russian orchestral repertoire, played and replayed across the country. In March 1938 Arthur Toscanini gave the first American performance in New York, where its reception mirrored a telling division within the American left. Those who accepted the Popular Front consensus hailed the symphony as a representation of the Communist utopia. Those left-wing socialists and Trotskyites who had been disillusioned by the show-trials and saw the Russian leader as a Red Wizard of Oz, a sly illusionist, were more disposed to hear its satirical, subversive edge.

Not so in the Soviet Union. As Stalin cemented his monolithic hegemony by eliminating the last of the Trotskyite opposition at home, Shostakovich's *yurodivy* gesture seemed to have been taken not so much at face value – since its face value was unmistakably negative – but with an almost mystical transvaluation. From whatever source, word went about that the renegade had created a fine and acceptable work and now seemed to be toeing the line. The famous superscription confirmed it. It was, however, widely known that the words were not the composer's own. Not long before the Moscow premiere, a newspaper reported that "Creative reply of a Soviet musician to just criticism" was a phrase suggested to Shostakovich by an unidentified journalist. The story went on to say that the composer had "gratefully" agreed with the words. On such shifting sands are personal mythologies constructed.

Shostakovich was now at least partially insulated by fame. In contrast to the inconsistently translated poets and novelists who had disappeared during the purges, he enjoyed international fame, his music part of the *lingua franca* of pre-war liberalism. His arrest and liquidation would have sparked an international outcry. He was also confirmed as professor at Leningrad Conservatory. In December 1939 he was elected to the Leningrad City Soviet.

All this called for some reciprocal creative gesture. Shrewdly, Shostakovich announced that his next major project was to be a symphony inspired by Mayakovsky's poem *V I Lenin*, ostensibly to be played on Stalin's 60th birthday. There could hardly be a creative gesture more politically correct and flattering than to underline the apostolic continuity between the Founding Father and the *Vozhd*, and to do it using an officially canonised poet and text. In addition, Shostakovich undertook a new orchestration of *Boris Godunov* by the revered Mussorgsky, finished in 1940 but not heard for another twenty years.

The latter project was a labour of love, with its deeply democratic message and its prophetic vision of "Darkness, impenetrable darkness"; the former as blatant a smokescreen as *From Karl Marx to Our Own Days* had been in 1932. At the very moment Shostakovich seemed to have pulled himself together and wakened to his reponsibilities as a People's Artist – as Prokofiev was doing at the time – his real work took on an inward and private cast. As deadlines came and went for the largely mythical "Lenin" Symphony, Shostakovich turned to chamber music. He even abandoned a projected opera. Two of the three major pieces written before the beginning of what in the Soviet Union was known as the Great Patriotic War were for small instrumental groups. There was also a new symphony, but it was as unlike the promised choral work as could be imagined and again it laid Shostakovich open to criticism,

As there were between the *Four Pushkin Romances* and the Fifth Symphony, there are clear similarities between Shostakovich's First Quartet and his Sixth Symphony, the same coded continuity. It was not strictly true that, as he claimed, Shostakovich had not previously written for string quartet. Some earlier pieces derived from the *Lady Macbeth* score and *The Golden Age* were found after his death. The form was not widely revered in Russia, where the symphony, opera and the ballet were regarded as the major forms for a classical composer. And yet, no less than with the fifteen symphonies, Shostakovich transformed his country's perception of the form with the same number of quartets, a cycle that managed to combine epic sweep with the most penetrating inscape.

The String Quartet No 1 in C, Op 49 was not perhaps the most promising or auspicious start to the sequence. It is almost deliberately backward looking. Shostakovich tried to minimise its importance by referring to it as a mere exercise, but its autobiographical components – personal grief, idyllic memories of childhood at Irinovka – are hard to miss, and yet like the symphony that followed, the quartet seems curiously drained of feeling, unlike those intensely confessional quartets by Janáček, Smetana and Dvořák which had taken the cue of Beethoven's last great sequence of chamber music and used the string quartet not just as a technical challenge but as an emotional plumb-line.

The success of the First Quartet brought Shostakovich an immediate request from the Beethoven Quartet, who had premiered it, for a work which they could play alongside the composer. The Piano Quintet in G minor, Op 57 won Shostakovich the Stalin Prize. In sequence it followed his work on *Boris Godunov* and the Sixth Symphony and assimilated elements of both within a brilliantly executed classical structure. The Sixth Symphony is another problematic work, the two fast movements hanging like sarcastic appendages from the huge opening slow movement, which is subtantially longer than the other two put together. There is some evidence that it attempts to convey Shostakovich's state of mind following the Composers' Union lynching of February 1936. It has the same stillness and plainness which marked the First Quartet, and which troubled those critics who required a "Socialist Realist" symphony to spark and fizz. How much that monochrome quality was the result of exhaustion and relief, how much to a deliberate decision to simplify the means is open to question. It has been proposed that the simplicity of the First Quartet was due to the birth of Shostakovich's son Maxim in May 1938. The boy's arrival may have set the father thinking again about his own lost childhood, but the notion of Shostakovich writing simple music with one hand while rocking a cradle with the other absurdly misunderstands the absoluteness of his absorption in any musical project, or whatever scale.

The vagaries, negative and positive, of his last two symphonies had left him written out, somewhat as he had been after the First. He was also aware that he was expected to deliver a vast choral symphony, and to some degree the chamber pieces were temporising manoeuvres, written as an excuse for the non-appearance of the "Lenin". The Piano Quintet and the Sixth Symphony also form an important pair in that the same uneasy balance of tragedy and satire is maintained. The leverage is rather different in each case. The symphony tends to hold the two moods in ambivalent opposition, giving the later movements their slightly hysterical, cast, reminiscent of fairground music. In the Quintet, Shostakovich is closer to integrating them. Given that this was a work in which he would also have a hand as performer, its importance is beyond question and it remains one of the most popular of his chamber works, albeit inconsistently and often inaccurately played.

The Sixth Symphony was premiered in early November 1938. It would attract harsh criticism from the Composers' Union, but only some 20 months later. By then, though, wider events were in the saddle. The Great Terror had limped to an end, with an inevitable change at the head of the NKVD. Yezhov was discovered to have been plotting Stalin's assassination. His replacement Lavrenti Beria was to become an icon of Communist decadence, a kerb-crawling pervert whose only loyalties were to Stalin and to his own convenience. Leon Trotsky's death warrant had long since been signed, and the contract was fulfilled on August 20 1940, in Mexico. At home, Maxim Litvinov, the commissar for foreign affairs, who had secured US recognition of the Soviet Union in 1934, was replaced by Vyacheslav Molotov in May 1939. As well as lending his (assumed) surname to a favourite guerrilla weapon, Molotov's great achievement was to negotiate the diabolic accord that in August of that year "guaranteed" non-aggression between the Soviet Union and the National Socialist government in Berlin and in the process allowed Germany and Russia to divide Poland between them and Russia to strengthen her Western approaches by invading Finland, and then the three Baltic republics.

In following the Fifth Symphony with a work as introverted and opaquely straighforward as the Sixth, Shostakovich may have invited trouble. As it turned out, by the time his peers gathered to accuse him of recidivism, the Nazi-Soviet pact had been torn up and for the second time in Shostakovich's lifetime, his country was at war. It was to provide a ironic respite.

Chapter Five

Когда я ночью жду ее прихода,
Жизнь, кажется, висит на волоске.
Что почести, что юность, что свобода
Пред милой гостьей с дудочкой в
руке.

И вот вошла. Откинув покрывало,
Внимательно взглянула на меня.
Ей говорю: "Ты ль Данту диктовала

Chapter Five

On June 22 1941, Hitler unleashed Operation Barbarossa on the Soviet Union. The devils' pact was broken. Taking a cue and a codeword from his imagined predecessor the Holy Roman Emperor Frederick "Redbeard", the Nazi leader set out to conquer the whole of Western Russia and the Ukraine and to set the eastern borders of the Third Reich on a line from Arkhangel on the White Sea to Astrakhan on the Black. Early progress was swift. The purging in June 1937 of Shostakovich's friend Marshal Tukhachevsky and some 80,000 other military personnel, including senior strategic cadres, seriously compromised Soviet resistance, adding weight to the suggestion that the Gestapo had been involved in the military "plot" against Stalin. The Red Army created by Leon Trotsky was still a formidable fighting force, but deployed across the largest theatre ever seen in modern warfare, its organisational shortcomings were potentially fatal.

The Eastern Front became a byword for brutality, its long bitter stalemates and sieges – of Stalingrad most notoriously – were as bloody as any between 1914 and 1918. No one knows how many Russians died during the "Fascist War" or the "Great Patriotic War" (as the conflict is known in Russia) but added to the millions shot, starved and exiled during the Terror the losses might well seem biblical and apocalyptic. However, it is mistaken to think that the war was the greater disaster. Twice as many Russians died at Stalin's hands than at Hitler's, a bitter irony that would in due course be found coded in the conflict's most famous music. On the positive side, though, the war afforded a new sense of national purpose and, for artists and intellectuals who had attracted unwelcome attention from the regime, a certain breathing space. In her oral and textual biography of Shostakovich, Elizabeth Wilson surprisingly heads her chapter on the war years, "A Respite".

On the face of it, it must have seemed a very tough respite. Leningrad was within reach of the Nazi lightning bolt, sandwiched between the German Army Group North and the smaller but no less passionate Finnish Army, fired with memories of the November 1939 Soviet invasion. Winter warfare would prove the undoing of the German Army, but summer conditions eased the crossing of the Dvina and the swift rolling-up of the Baltic republics. By August, Leningrad was under siege.

In the summer of 1941, Professor D D Shostakovich was grading his composition students at the Conservatoire. He was, however, anxious to serve the Motherland and applied to enlist in a home defence unit. His extreme myopia unfitted him for active service, but he was accepted as an auxiliary fireman and began to write musical arrangments – like *The Fearless Regiments Are On The Move* – for performance at the front. The authorities made sure that Shostakovich was seen to be doing his patriotic duty. He was photographed firewatching on the Conservatoire roof, plying a hose and wearing the helmet that would give the composer such a strange and almost comic presence on the cover of *Time* magazine. He also made a morale-boosting broadcast on Radio Leningrad, as did the formerly proscribed poet Anna Akhmatova.

Conditions in Leningrad were increasingly severe, however, as bombing gradually destroyed the city's infrastructure and the siege, which was to last nearly a year and a half, took a hold on its inhabitants. On October 1 1941, a week after a frugal 35th birthday party, Shostakovich, Nina, Galina and three year old Maxim were evacuated to Moscow by aircraft. His mother and sister Maria remained for the moment in Leningrad, but were evacuated the following spring. Given the military situation, with the Wehrmacht and Panzer divisions in reach of the overcrowded and chaotic capital, and with frontline gunfire clearly audible, it was decided the family should move still further east. After a fortnight in Moscow, they boarded a train bound for Sverdlovsk, the industrial and cultural capital of the Ural region. The city had been renamed in 1924 and in honour of the Bolshevik leader Yakov Sverdlov. Prior to that, it had been known as Ekaterinburg, infamous as the final resting place of Tsar Nicholas II and his family, murdered there at the "House of Special Purpose" on July 17 1918.

In the event, the Shostakoviches did not get as far as Sverdlovsk. There are poignant stories of the composer, looking sad and distracted, standing on the station platform in Leningrad with a sewing machine in one hand and a child's pot in the other; later, of him washing plates in the snow beside the train. Fellow-evacuees advised Shostakovich to travel on to Tashkent where food was plentiful, and where many of the Conservatoire staff and students were already relocated. After a gruelling week on the train, constantly being shunted aside to give priority to troop and hospital transports and relieved only by the company of his composer friend Vissarion Shebalin, Shostakovich decided that the family should disembark in Kuibyshev on the Volga. This was Russia's war capital, renamed after Politburo member Valerian Kuibyshev, who had died in 1935. Now once again Samara, the city's leading tourist attraction is Stalin's strategic bunker; composer and *Vozhd* seemed bound together by some curious magnetism.

The family were initially processed and given rough accommodation in one of the city's schools. They were then offered a small flat (with rickety upright piano) at 140 ul. Frunze where Shostakovich was at least able to work and to draw rations from the commissariat at the Bolshoi Theatre. On March 11 1942, the family was moved to more spacious accommodation at 2a ul. Vilonovskaya. By then, Shostakovich was on the brink of his greatest fame, for a week before the premiere of his Seventh Symphony, destined to become his most celebrated work, had been given in Kuibyshev. The symphony's subsequent history was extraordinary, so much so that an almost mythical reputation has clouded the circumstances of its creation.

It is generally assumed that the Symphony No 7 in C, Op 60 *To the City of Leningrad* was written in direct response to the sufferings of the composer's birthplace during the siege. Shostakovich had perhaps cemented this misconception by announcing during his Radio Leningrad broadcast that he was at work on a new symphony, a decision considered heroically optimistic by many of his listeners. The work was in fact conceived before the Nazi invasion. Anything written in *Testimony* can reasonably be suspected of *arrière-pensée* but the claims of that strange, bitter text have to be taken seriously and in it Shostakovich was clear that the sorrow and the feelings of solidarity he expresses in the Seventh Symphony were for the sufferings of the people of Leningrad not just under several months of Nazi bombardment but under fifteen years of Stalinism.

However subtly encrypted the symphony's message, and however camouflaged by official propaganda, Shostakovich was still treading a dangerous line. The Sixth Symphony had met with official displeasure for its Formalist/individualist elements, but had appealed to concert audiences presumably tired of endless affirmative song-symphonies, like Shebalin's ultra-"proletarian" *Lenin*. Even more dangerous, though, was the kind of reception Shostakovich began to receive after the Fifth Symphony. Audience response to his Piano Quintet effectively clapped out of countenance the regime's suspicion that chamber music, with its bourgeois and again individualistic overtones, was inappropriate in the Communist paradise. It looked for a time as though Shostakovich and his fans were driving cultural policy, not Stalin and the Politburo. A decade after the nadir of his *Lenin Symphony,* Shebalin was writing string quartets, as was Nicholas Myaskovsky, while Prokofiev forged ahead with set-aside chamber works.

There was danger as well as benefit in the applause. Shostakovich found himself in the excruciating position of receiving rapturous welcomes from fellow-composers whenever he turned up at meetings, this at a time when only one man in the Soviet Union was entitled to a standing ovation, and that was the Beloved Leader. Shostakovich was one of the few Russian composers of any note who had failed to produce a 60th birthday eulogy to the "Wisest of the Wise". Stalin must, however, have recognised that Shostakovich's propaganda value outweighed any embarrassing heterodoxy and awkward fame. Since the disastrous reverse at Vyazma, the only urgent priority was keeping Hitler from the gates of Moscow, and besides, Stalin must have felt that in Kuibyshev he could keep close tabs on his errant composer, and if need be dispose of him. The Volga was deep, and old Samara had always been regarded as the gateway to Siberia.

Shostakovich had begun serious work on the Seventh Symphony in late July 1941. Within a month, he had completed the massive opening movement. He began the second just as the Nazi bombardment began but despite his Civil Defence duties and the terrifying noise – which later entered the sound-world of his greatest string quartet – he finished it, too, in just two weeks; Shostakovich always had the ability

to concentrate in the most distracting of circumstances. On the day he made his Radio Leningrad broadcast, he played through the finished parts to a group of friends. He did the same when he arrived in Moscow, at the home of Aram Khachaturian, whose First Symphony was on the same programme as Shostakovich's Fifth at its premiere.

A soldier buying tickets for the performance of the Seventh Symphony in Leningrad in 1943 became one of the most enduring images of the besieged city.

The now half-finished score and the manuscript of *Lady Macbeth of Mtsensk* were among the few personal possessions Shostakovich took with him from Leningrad. He resumed work on the symphony in Kuibyshev, which must have given a homesick inflection to its inscription, finishing the score two days after Christmas 1941. There were immediate plans to put the new work into rehearsal. Mravinsky and the Leningrad Philharmonic had been evacuated to Novosibirsk, which would have presented severe logistical problems, so, on March 5 1942, in Kuibyshev, Samuel Samosud conducted the first performance with the Bolshoi Theatre Orchestra. It was met with huge acclaim. Copies of the score were smuggled out of the Soviet Union on microfilm. Arthur Toscanini conducted the Seventh Symphony at Radio City. A month before, on June 22, Henry Wood, founder of the London Proms, gave the first British performance which was attended by this writer's father, an experience he remembered for the rest of his life. A shortwave radio fanatic, he remembered with even greater clarity and passion hearing the Seventh Symphony broadcast from Russia. On March 29 1942 Grigori Stolyarov had given the second performance in Moscow during an air-raid. The event was transmitted worldwide.

The *Leningrad* Symphony, as it was universally known, became a powerful symbol of wartime resistance. More important symbolically, and certainly of greater emotional importance to Shostakovich, was a performance in the city that had inspired the work.

It is probably the only time in musical history that military operations were coordinated to assist an orchestral concert. In what was known as "Operation Squall", Leningrad's military commander launched a bombardment of German positions designed to quieten the guns long enough for the work to unfold uninterrupted; a detail that makes the occasional bleep of cellphones and winter coughs at concerts seem absurdly trivial interruptions. It is probably also the only known occasion when recruitment posters called not for soldiers to serve the Motherland but for musicians. The score had been flown in on a medical transport, but there was no active orchestra left in Leningrad, and certainly not one large enough to perform a work that required huge forces, equivalent to the massed sound of the Fourth Symphony. The Philharmonic was far to the East and the surviving members of the Radio Orchestra – not much more than a dozen out of the original hundred or so – were in a parlous condition, raddled with hunger and dysentery like everyone else in the city. The conductor Karl Eliasberg (who seems to have dropped the second half of his German-sounding name) was so ill that he collapsed while walking home from rehearsals. In an echo of what had happened to Shostakovich during the hunger years of the Civil War, he was granted extra rations and a bed at Philharmonic Hall. The orchestra players, too, were given food out of a fast-dwindling supply.

Even so, it was a motley collection of old men, musically literate infantrymen plucked from the front-line and a few professionals who gave the *Leningrad* its apotheosis on August 9. Not even the first performance of Olivier Messaien's *Quartet for the End of Time* in a German Stalag on broken instruments and in front of an audience of several thousand (that is the version of legend; the instruments were almost certainly sound, if rudimentary, and those attending at Gorlitz probably numbered no more than a few hundred) has such a powerful emotional resonance.

The Seventh Symphony is scored for a very large orchestra, with heavily reinforced brasses and percussion. Though his later comments seem to contradict it, Shostakovich gave a programme note which relates the Seventh quite explicitly to the war.

Allegretto – Suddenly war breaks into our peaceful lives. Perhaps the most famous passage in the whole of Shostakovich's music, and the most celebrated of his marches, is signalled by a half-heard side-drum whose tattoo cuts across the almost bucolic opening, played by strings, bassoons and winds, leading to a beautiful violin melody. The march rises to a shocking crescendo, with percussion and extra brasses adding to the onslaught. The juggernaut passes, leaving flutes and violins, and a surviving bassoon from the opening pages, to stagger disoriented towards the climax. There is, however, hope in this, some determination to keep alive the music of the opening. Violins and flute rework that same material, transforming it into something celebratory that manages to defy the ever-present martial threat.

Moderato (poco allegretto) – Memories. If this looks back to the past as the programme suggests, it is here where Shostakovich may make the most explicit connection between the "Leningrad that Stalin destroyed" and the city "that Hitler merely finished off". The opening melody is far from nostalgic. It has a restless quality, developed by second violins and soon joined by low strings and woodwinds. There then comes a bizarre waltz, its wild eroticism a reference perhaps to the days of total sexual licence after the Revolution. Another march cuts across it before the movement ended in an oddly chastened spirit.

Adagio – Our Country's wide vistas. This was the heart of the symphony according to Shostakovich. It begins with a plain wind theme, underpinned by harps, which is Russian to its core. Having established his landscape, Shostakovich then peoples it in an intense string melody that gradually draws in strings and harp again. There is a storm, but whether natural or man-made isn't clear, though the latter is hinted at in a quiet side-drum part. It is as if Shostakovich is saying that Russia has weathered adversity and invasion for much of its history, an endless cycle signalled by the repeated and transformed opening material that comes back in soft woodwinds and plucked strings at the end, with a tam-tam suggesting the country's beating heart.

Allegro non troppo – Victory and a beautiful life in the future. The finale is played *attacca,* without a break, opening with muted strings and a faint roll of thunder in the distance. Vernacular voices call back and forth on horns and oboes, but there is intense purpose in this closing movement as well, trumpets and strings in rugged solidarity. Their determination simply grows, in apparent obedience to some relentless historical logic that beats away underneath. The logic of its C major tonality, the classical key of affirmation, becomes clear at the end, as percussion joins in what sounds less like a victory celebration than some ritual of rededication.

The Seventh Symphony lasts one hour and a quarter, but seems to touch on a far longer cycle of history.

The backlash was quick and powerful, in the West at least. In a matter of eighteen months, the Leningrad Symphony had supplanted Jean Sibelius's Second Symphony (a surprise choice, but one confirmed by pre-war ballots) as the favourite of American concert-goers. Once the euphoria of those early performances had worn off, and the dramatic context forgotten, American critics began to condemn the Seventh Symphony as a work of propaganda, overblown and rhetorical. By the end of the war, and for many years thereafter, it was rarely performed in America, and only somewhat more often in the United Kingdom. Only in Russia did it retain its former authority.

Perversely, though, Shostakovich seemed bent on engineering a personal backlash at home. The Honoured Artist of the RSFSR must have seemed immune to criticism after the triumph of the Seventh. It successor, though, was to be one of his most problematic works. Recognised now as one of his greatest achievements, the Eighth Symphony also disappeared from the Western concert repertoire immediately after the war and never received more than a lukewarm reception in the Soviet Union. However, during the cultural if not political thaw of the 1960s, the Eighth assumed a new significance in the West which it has borne until very recently, when again its perceived shortcomings have assumed priority.

The end of 1942 saw Shostakovich again seriously ill, this time with gastric typhoid. He spent some time in a sanatorium near Moscow, able to work on nothing more substantial than the Second Piano Sonata, a bitter, enervated work that again foregrounds Shostakovich's satiric side. He had also, the day after writing the final cadences of the Seventh Symphony, begun work on a third opera, *The Gamblers*, never finished, but apparently written in a similar, sarcastic spirit. Shostakovich had languished in Kuibyshev and planned to travel to Novosibirsk to be with Mravinsky and his friend Sollertinsky, but Shebalin, the new director of the Moscow Conservatoire, offered him a chair in composition. In April 1943, Shostakovich and Nina returned to the capital.

The children, for the moment, remained by the Volga. Though danger was ever-present, Russian fortunes in the war had turned. "General Winter" had proved to be the decisive commander. The siege of Leningrad was eased, though more than half a million of the city's inhabitants had died of starvation, and the suffering would continue for another year. On February 2, the siege at Stalingrad ended with the German surrender and the Soviet Union began to counter-attack. In July, just as Shostakovich was beginning the Eighth Symphony, Russian and German armour clashed at Kursk in an almost medieval joust that altered the course of the Eastern Front. By the time the Eighth Symphony was premiered in Moscow, the Allied leaders – Churchill, Roosevelt, Stalin – were preparing to meet in Tehran, this two years before the more celebrated Yalta conference, to discuss the disposition of the post-war world.

The Symphony No 8 in C minor, Op 65 was written in just ten weeks, between July 1 and September 9 1943, and largely at the new Composers' Colony at Ivanovo. For some critics, the speed of composition is reflected in a drastic loss of technical – or possibly emotional – control. Ian MacDonald suggests that Shostakovich "blew a fuse" and produced an "earthbound" work that lacks the "vital electricity" that set him apart from almost all of his contemporaries. This smacks of what another observer Christopher Norris calls "ideological reaction" and it is also coloured by a particular hindsight.

As gramophone recordings became increasingly important in the post-war period, interpretations of Shostakovich's work were increasingly coloured by performance values, and by the vagaries of interpretation. Successive conductors took sizeable liberties with the composer's expressive and rhythmic markings. Recordings of the Eighth are wildly variable in duration. The composer's son Maxim Shostakovich turned it into a dark personal odyssey and stretched the symphony out to some seventy minutes. Bychkov's version with the Berlin Philharmonic reduces the work to a sequence of bleakly nihilistic fragments and slows the first and last movement unbearably. Bernard Haitink seems to have intuited the work's tightly organised symphonic argument and brings it in at around the hour mark, an astonishing variation. Only the trusted Mravinsky, who had visited Shostakovich at Ivanovo during the writing of the piece and may have influenced the upbeat Allegretto finale with his enthusiasm for the first four movements, seems able to balance dramatic and structural values and to produce a recording both emotionally satisfying and faithful to Shostakovich's intentions.

Because the Eighth Symphony exists as a complex of antagonistic interpretations, it can be difficult to describe neutrally. Certain details are incontestable. The work is dominated by a huge Adagio opening movement, which is twice the length of the finale and four times as long as movements two and three. However, the architectural balance of the piece is achieved by playing the last three movements without a break, a device Shostakovich returned to in the Ninth Symphony and in the string quartets.

The Adagio begins in the home key of C minor, a tonality that might recall the "fate" motto of Beethoven's Third Symphony or Schubert's Fourth, known as "Tragic". The lower strings establish a strong dotted phrase that gives the work a deceptively vehement beginning, and perhaps suggests that it begins *in media re*, as if the symphonies from No 5 onwards really were part of an epic cycle. This gives way to a softer theme, immediately reminiscent of the opening movement of the Fifth. Shostakovich instructed that the strings bow *sul tasto*, or above the fingerboard, a device that bleaches the sound-colour considerably. There is a throat-clearing interlude for the lower woodwinds before the second subject gets under way. Violins play robustly over a steady string pulse with violas and cor anglais emphasizing a sanguine and apparently optimistic mood.

With a return to the nervous opening figure, the flutes suggest that all is not as it seems. A militaristic drum beat establishes a note of urgency, though the basic pulse remains constant. There is an abrupt, powerful climax that completes the dynamic gamut from a near-inaudible *pppp* at the start of the violin melody to a stunning *ffff* as the central conflict breaks. Suddenly up a gear, the woodwinds bleat ominously, while at some distance from the main action, the horns and cellos sound distant warnings of disaster. A heavy-footed march follows and it is hard not to picture the trumpets and glockenspiels of Nazi bands at Nuremburg. This "bloated and unfocused mess" ends with a plaintive cor anglais solo which MacDonald, not in any way disposed to hear the virtues of the Eighth, considers "interminable". The end of the Adagio is no longer and says no more than it needs to.

The second movement is a scherzo with a surprisingly dour aspect. It recalls Shostakovich's more obviously satirical writing, but seems to have moved a step beyond merely guying Fascist goose steps to launch a more general attack on extremism of thought and the failure of intellectual generosity. The composer makes considerable use of widely spaced woodwind pitches over a basic D flat tonality that is determinedly unsymphonic and banal in character.

It is almost certain that the sound effects and battering ostinatos of the E minor third movement are intended to suggest military conflict. There are shell-bursts, machine gun fire, panicky musters and urgent high-pitched trumpet calls, but again the onomatopoeic character of the music always seems prepared to be drawn up into something larger. In place of juxtaposition, Shostakovich allows the dissonant conclusion to dissolve into the succeeding Largo, which represents the heart of the closing meta-movement. It is cast as a passacaglia, a set of polyphonic variations over a ground bass and similar in form to the great interlude in *Lady Macbeth of Mtsensk*. Stage by stage, the music is transformed from bleak defeatism (every phrase abruptly shut off or wearily attenuated) to a level of philosophical confidence that is

A still from a documentary on Shostakovich filmed in 1966

too guarded and carefully mediated to characterize as optimism.

The ending is unexpectedly affirmative. It opens with a parping bassoon melody which sets in motion a sequence of languid philosophical discussions drawing in violins, a flute, cellos and oboes. There are quotations from earlier movements and from other works, notably the Piano Quintet, with its betrayal motif. It has become customary to hear the conclusion as devoid of animation, but it sounds more like the gesture of a composer who has already completed his argument and just spends a moment or two listening to it circulating, not quite reliably, round its orchestral "audience".

The radicalism of the Eighth Symphony is that it is a meditation on the whole idea of symphonism. MacDonald suggests that it "swings a sandbag against the listener's skull", but it is in many way the least histrionic of the wartime symphonies and a return to the modernist experiment of the equally unloved Fourth. There is far less inscape, far less newsreel, far less sound-tracking and special pleading than in its predecessors, and yet, simply experienced rather than interrogated from ideological premises, it tells far more about war, intolerance and suffering than almost anything else Shostakovich ever wrote.

Whether it was less about the war years than about the pre-war sufferings of the Russian people, as Shostakovich suggested in *Testimony*, is difficult to judge in hindsight. But certainly its apparently tragic tone was sharply at odds with the mood of national optimism that followed changing military fortunes. Shostakovich was entirely aware of this. About a month after the premiere, Shostakovich wrote to Glikman, telling him that a Composers' Union meeting to discuss the work had been cancelled because he was unwell, but that he looked forward to the criticisms of his colleagues which would surely – as they had with the Fifth Symphony – spur him to greater creativity; "instead of one step backwards, I will make one step forwards". The letter drips with sarcasm.

The authorities tried to pass the Eighth Symphony off as a memorial to the dead of Stalingrad, thus justifying its sombre character by turning it into Shostakovich's Requiem; he uses the analogy himself in *Testimony*, of the Seventh and Eighth together, but with a sharply different emphasis. It was harder to find a rationalisation for the Ninth Symphony's apparent refusal to celebrate victory in the Great Patriotic War. As he had done before, Shostakovich told the press he was working on just such a piece, but in *Testimony* he commented bitterly that "they wanted a fanfare from me, an ode...and they demanded that Shostakovich use quadruple winds, choir and soloists to hail the leader. All the more because Stalin found the number nine auspicious..." Shostakovich, of course, had another reason for considering it in the opposite light. Were he to end *his* Ninth Symphony with a vast apotheosis, it would invite unsupportable comparison with the great Choral Symphony of Beethoven. Stalin might be satisfied with the comparison; Shostakovich's fellow-composers would use it to mock him. It may also be that having written upbeat wartime pieces and undemanding fodder for the NKVD Music and Dance Ensemble [sic!], that having collaborated with Khachaturian on *The Song of the Red Army* for the National Anthem competition, he considered his patriotic duty done for the present.

The desire for privacy, the need to claw back some personal space for private meditation, had been sharpened by grief. Sollertinsky, perhaps his greatest friend, died suddenly in February 1944. The hope that they might work happily together in Moscow evaporated in a moment. Shostakovich poured his sadness into the Piano Trio No 2 in E minor, Op 67, a work that begins in unbearable desolation and ends in a brutal *danse macabre* as Shostakovich and all Russians watched the unfolding horror of the Nazi death camps, progressively "liberated" as the German line rolled backwards. He may have wanted private space, but for Shostakovich history always pushed at the door. That is also unexpectedly true of his String Quartet No 2 in A, Op 68, also finished in 1944, shortly after Galina and Maxim were returned to the family in Moscow. It is the absolute opposite of its predecessor, massive, dark, almost symphonic, and full of satire, just like the Ninth Symphony.

Stalin had wanted an apotheosis. Shostakovich gave him "just music" as he wryly commented of the Ninth, but it is music that encodes some of his fiercest and most damaging caricatures of the leader. The music is full of brutal lockstep figures, which by now always seem to herald the arrival of the *Vozhd,* and sharp-eared listeners will detect a curious Wagnerian tinge, apparently a reference to the kinship-in-hell of the two dictators who between them had just accounted for some twenty-five or thirty million souls. The Symphony No 9 in E flat major, Op 70 is not Shostakovich's greatest work, but it is not the slight and baffling trifle that is sometimes suggested. Shostakovich knew what he was in for long before the premiere. The now familiar two-piano reduction had given the Composers Union time to sharpen its collective knives. The respite was over.

Chapter Six

Chapter Six

Shostakovich wrote very little music in 1946. There is no need to invent a *crise de quarante*. He may have been approaching his 40th birthday, but he was tired and weakened by disease and after the bruising encounters of the previous ten years, his natural instinct was retreat. The family spent the summer at Komarova, outside Leningrad. In subsequent years, they occupied apartments in a dacha owned by Nina's father. It was decided not to move back permanently to Leningrad itself, though his mother and sister did. Though Shostakovich continued as professor in the Conservatoire, he also had a post in Moscow, and at the beginning of 1947, the Shostakoviches moved into a new flat in the capital.

There were more pressing objective reasons for his silence than academic duties and family upheaval. The end of the war laid a pall of ambiguity over the Soviet Union. Former allies were already declared enemies. Members of the Red Army unfortunate enough to have been captured were brought home – many against their will – and immediately liquidated. Any contact with the West was considered a dangerous contagion, punishable by death or deportation to the Gulag. Given such a drastic transvaluation, even writers and composers eager to mollify the regime could not know what position to take, or what literary sources to employ. The discovery that a certain Russian writer was admired in the West would be enough to guarantee his proscription and an uncertain fate for anyone aligned with him. Shostakovich found himself in this position when he wrote soundtrack music (only the second significant score of 1946) for Kozintsev's and Trauberg's *Simple Folk* only to find the film condemned as "un-Soviet, anti-patriotic and anti-People". In such an atmosphere the song-symphonies dried up; opera stalled; only once-suspect chamber music and instrumental works were considered safe.

Shostakovich's String Quartet No 3 in F, Op 73 was largely finished at Komarova, and seems to have cost its creator dear. The man who could produce vast orchestral scores at lightning speed struggled to finish it. There was nothing new in the structure. Indeed, the trajectory of the quartet is identical to that of the Seventh Symphony and the other wartime works, with a peaceful, almost folksy opening cut across by a sardonic scherzo, then plunged into what can only be interpreted as grief (another powerful passacaglia) before ending ambiguously. It is thought that the slow movement, worked on while Shostakovich visited his mother, bears marks of his distress at Leningrad's shattered cityscape.

The quartet's unmissable numerological code – two against three, Stalin against People – is again familiar from previous works. And again Shostakovich provided the work with a programme note which attempted to pass it off as a simple memory of the late war, and the ambiguity of the last movement as a moral and philosophical question: why? Even here, though, his real intentions were not far from the surface. Were the "rumblings of unrest and anticipation" in the opening movement really just pre-war fears and nerves (Stalin had apparently ignored warnings of an impending Nazi attack) or did they point to something more subversive?

There were rumbles of unrest inside the Soviet monolith, suicidal uprisings in the Gulag, and the deep destructive rumble that would haunt the later 20th century was heard for the first time, down in the basses, as the Soviet Union embarked on her own nuclear programme. The "Iron Curtain" described by Winston Churchill at Fulton, Missouri, in March 1946 had clashed shut, but in Stalin's mind the "Cold War" had already begun.

While Americans searched inventively for Reds under the beds and Communists in the State Department, the Soviet regime began smoking out "Formalists" again. "Socialist Realism" was back in the saddle, and every bit as capricious and amorphous as it had been before. There was a Red Queen logic to the term: it meant exactly what Stalin said it meant, or in more practical terms what his cultural enforcer said it meant. Russia was entering "the Time of Zhdanov", or *Zhdanovshchina*. The new cultural commissar was a former Party boss in Leningrad, and thus already familiar to Shostakovich. A hoodlum whose viciousness increased sharply in the presence of beauty and intelligence, Andrei Zhdanov pulls off the extraordinary historical trick of making Senator Joseph McCarthy look like Solomon, and the rabid editor of *Die Sturmer* Julius Streicher like Savonarola.

Not only was Zhdanov a philistine, he was an anti-Semite as well. The cultural paranoia of *Zhdanovshchina* seemed to have breathed in the poisonous smoke of the Holocaust. Much as Hitler had done in *Mein Kampf* with respect to the Western Front in the First World War, Stalin began to see the Jews behind Russia's wartime reverses in the Second. He and Zhdanov also made the same equation of Jewry and modernism, which was only another, deceivingly positive term for "Formalism".

Shostakovich seems at first to have been relatively sanguine, or at least fatalistic, about this latest clamp-down. "I had gone through it at a younger age and the subsequent storms and bad weather had hardened me", he suggests in *Testimony*. After the Eighth and Ninth Symphonies, the *yurodivy* mask must have seemed full of holes, but perhaps experience had simply given Shostakovich another layer of skin. There are other reasons why he could afford to be philosophical. He hadn't written much music in 1946. If there were no new scores, there was nothing to criticise; there also seemed to be less pressure to produce propaganda works. By the spring of 1947, Shostakovich's non-musical workload had also risen. In addition to his teaching responsibilities, which called for regular travel between the capital and Leningrad, he was appointed Chairman of the Leningrad Composers' Union; irony of ironies in view of what had happened there and what was just about to. A short time afterward, in the summer of 1947, Shostakovich was appointed a deputy to the Supreme Soviet of the RSFSR, an essentially meaningless role that mostly involved passing on edicts from Stalin and the Central Committee, but again a time-consuming one. Perhaps the government was playing its version of the *yurodivy* game: identify the trouble-maker, but instead of punishing him, make him part of the system and keep watch that way instead. Also, the more files and directives Shostakovich had to read and initial, the fewer "dissident" works he might write.

There was one further reason why Shostakovich might initially have regarded Zhdanov's reign with some equanimity. It was clear that literature was the primary target. The regime reserved its harshest criticism for Boris Pasternak, who had embarked on *Dr Zhivago*, but in secret, and for the poet Anna Akhmatova, a revered figure whose *Anno Domini MCMXI* had been published the year Shostakovich began writing music seriously, but whose great *Requiem* was not published in Russia until 1987. Akhmatova had been criticised and excluded before but her reputation remained untarnished. In May 1944 she gave a reading in Moscow, at which there was a spontaneous ovation; Stalin, who claimed sole right to such acclaim, was convinced that it had been organised. Akhmatova became an early target of Zhdanov's as a result and in August 1946 she and Mikhail Zoshchenko, author of *The Poker* and the autobiographical *Before Sunrise,* were humiliatingly expelled from the Writers' Union and "unpersoned". In contrast to Akhmatova – and to the stoical Shostakovich when he had been criticised at the height of the Terror – Zoshchenko was emotionally destroyed, reportedly begging friends to speak to him or even acknowledge his presence. (Akhmatova did later write the pro-Stalin *Glory to Peace* in hope of having her son freed from the Gulag, but the Great Leader was unforgiving.)

Shostakovich watched sympathetically. He must have been relieved when Zhdanov's next target was the cinema. Soviet film had iconic standing both at home as a symbol of Revolutionary progress away from the old bourgeois art forms, and abroad as an example of a radical art form developing its own new visual poetry. Nothing more thoroughly damned directors Vsevolod Pudovkin and even the great Sergei Eisenstein (for whose *Alexander Nevsky* Prokofiev had written a brilliant score) than that they were admired in America, Britain and France. It was, however, only a matter of time before Zhdanov's attention to the art form he understood least of all, and therefore most thoroughly suspected of unsoundness.

Science was his next target, leading to the Laputan nonsense of Lysenkoism in genetics, but in January 1948, the inevitable happened. Zhdanov chaired the First Congress of the Composers' Union in Moscow. It had all the hallmarks of a witch-hunt, with some elements of comedy theatre. Delegates laughed uproariously and self-consciously at Zhdanov's "jokes" and applied themselves with a will to the pre-arranged consensus. The ostensible target of criticism was the Georgian composer

Vano Muradeli, whose opera *The Great Friendship* was found to be infected with "Formalism" (read: had annoyed Stalin). Called to give an account of himself Muradeli gave the astonishing – and doubtless scripted – reply that Khachaturian, Myaskovsky, Prokofiev, and Shostakovich were all to blame for his work, because as the directorate of the Composers' Union they had turned "Formalism" into an orthodoxy which was hard to resist. "The Big Four" were subsequently removed from their posts in the directorate and replaced by nonentities. Criticism was extended to include Shebalin and Gavril Popov. As the assembly gave way to absurdity there seemed to be moves to declare all classical music redundant. In his closing comment at the first session Shostakovich simply made a plea for freedom of expression and fatalistically waited for judgement to be handed down. He didn't have long to wait. The following day he had to listen to the chairman describe his music as sounding like a pneumatic drill or a *dushegubka*, the latter a particularly chilling comparison since it refers to the specially adapted vans used by the Nazis to gas their victims. Having heard his work dismissed as a kind of hyper-naturalistic *musique concrète* Shostakovich simply thanked Comrade Zhdanov for a speech that would provide everyone with food for thought. It was an insincere vote of thanks from a condemned man, grating with sarcasm.

The absurdities of *Zhdanovshchina* were to appear – or rather to be concealed – in the secret cantata *Rayok* (or *Portrait Gallery*); some members of Shostakovich's circle claim to have seen or heard drafts of it in 1948, but it was probably written almost a decade later. In the event, Zhadnov would not be around long to haunt Shostakovich in person. At the end of August 1948, he fell ill and was unable to demonstrate his equally visionary grasp of other fields at the Soviet Congress of Agricultural Sciences. On the final day of the month, Zhdanov died. He had been a heavy drinker for some time, but there were suggestions that he had been poisoned. The idea was first mooted in 1953 during the so-called "Doctors' Plot" concocted to justify another round of terror during Stalin's last days, and it has since been suggested that Stalin himself was behind the assassination. The future Soviet leader Nikita Khrushchev describes in his memoir Stalin angrily warning Zhdanov about the perils of alcoholism. It was advice in the family, because the *Vozhd*'s daughter Svetlana Alliluyeva had married Zhadnov's son Yuri, but the show of concern might have been good cover, because Stalin was known to be enraged by Yuri's criticisms of "Lysenkoism".

Unfortunately for Shostakovich, Zhdanov's death merely brought to the fore a new tormentor. Composer Tikhon Khrennikov was a passionate and apparently sincere believer in the principles of Socialist Realism, though in *glasnost* days he claimed to have spoken and acted only as he did because of threats to his family. His Second Symphony of 1943 was an earnest expression of "the irresistible will to defeat the Fascist foe" and contained no individualist ambiguities whatsoever. At the end of the war, Khrennikov had served with the Red Army music corps and was in Berlin when the war ended. He joined the Communist Party in 1947 and was a deputy in the Supreme Soviet. He became secretary general of the Union of Soviet Composers during the purge which ousted the "Big Four" and held the post until 1987, when the last vestiges of old

Sovietism were finally dismantled. Driven by envy and spite (evident in his fury that the Seventh Symphony should have been likened to Comrade Beethoven) Khrennikov hounded Shostakovich and Prokofiev with particular fury and took a special delight in declaring their work unfit for performance and ordering that all recordings should be destroyed and scores pulped. Shostakovich's hatred – and his penchant for scatology –was evident when he put around the story (probably untrue) that Khrennikov had been so nervous while presenting a list of Stalin Prize nominees to the Great Leader–who could tell, day to day, which names were acceptable and which would damn a supporter to the farthest reaches of the Gulag? – that he had lost control of his bowels.

Shostakovich was not only once again unpersoned; his work was also airbrushed out of Russian musical history. The weeks following the Congress were awful. Following Zhdanov's formal announcement on February 10 he was forced to undergo a period of self-criticism and apology for what Khrennikov called the "frantically gloomy and neurotic" nature of his symphonies. Boris Pasternak was disgusted that Shostakovich (and Prokofiev, who wrote a letter of recantation) should not choose the path of silence. Outsiders, including Western critics, have been severally puzzled and profoundly disappointed that once again Shostakovich should have been made to toe the line. What they could not have understood, though Pasternak should, was the reality of Stalinist "criticism". Gangs of street children were organised to throw stones through the Shostakoviches' windows (Maxim remembers trying to repel the attacker with a catapult) while shouting the regime's stock insult. One thinks of Harrow schoolboys throwing stones at dachshunds in 1914, when anything German was suddenly anathema, but what did Muscovite street urchins understand by "Formalist"?

His troubles were not limited to sticks and stones. In September 1948 Shostakovich was dismissed from all his teaching posts for "professional incompetence", though in a perfect illustration of the regime's capriciousness, he was immediately appointed a People's Artist of the RSFSR. Stalin seemed inclined to keep Shostakovich close. The strings were pulled at will. Shostakovich was told that his *Poem of the Motherland*, written to mark the 30th anniversary of the Bolshevik Revolution was "inadequate" (it probably was), but Stalin personally approved his film music for Alexander Dovzhenko's *Michurin* and Grigori Alexandrov's *The Meeting on the Elbe*, significantly the two exceptions to an almost total Zhdanovist clampdown on movie-making in 1948.

Shostakovich was grateful for the income. Within eighteen months he would resume giving recitals in order to make ends meet. By then, though, he would have visited the United States as a delegate of the very men, Stalin and Khrennikov, who had declared his work unperformable at home and would have listened with a chill of understanding as the campaign against "Formalism" expressed itself afresh in a blunt proscription of "rootless cosmopolitans". The term barely needed decoding. Stalin had made anti-Semitism, something he had spoken out against in 1931, an instrument of state policy. At the height of the campaign, shortly before Stalin's death in 1953, Russians were warned that Jewish doctors were routinely injecting their patients with syphilis and cancerous cells and that the medicines they handed out were make of ground cockroaches. "The Doctors' Plot" was, unsuprisingly, a paranoid fiction cooked up by the MGB secret police.

Much has been said about the "Jewish" content of Shostakovich's First Violin Concerto. It was in fact one of a series of works which seemed to defy the edict by showing that Jewishness was, in fact, deeply rooted in Russian soil. It is important not to exaggerate the gesture of solidarity. To a large extent, the oppressed Jew stood as a convenient symbol for Shostakovich himself. He was also careful not to release these works at the time. The austere song cycle *From Jewish Folk Poetry,* Op 79, with its themes of privation and stoical survival, was not heard until 1955, some eight years after it was written, by which time of course Stalin was dead. The same applied to the String Quartet No 4 in D, Op 83. This was the last of the "Jewish" works, and again seems to follow the same dramatic logic of the wartime symphonies, beginning in folkish simplicity before its humane melodies are overpowered by snarling dissonances and further reminders of the "Stalin" motif.

The most important and self-revealing work of the sequence, though, is the Violin Concerto No 1 in A minor, Op 77. Written for the brilliant David Oistrakh, who made a speciality of the Beethoven concerto, it is a work again palpably haunted and nocturnal. Western critics and those who have happily swallowed the official representation of the war symphonies, have accepted that the First Violin Concerto is Shostakovich's response to the Holocaust. The fate of Europe's Jews and gypsies was clearly on his mind at this period – prompting memories of his father's love for *tsigany* songs, perhaps – but the concerto is also deeply and demonstrably autobiographical.

The opening movement again captures the atmosphere of sleepless anxiety Shostakovich felt during the Terror. The opening Nocturne has the colourless, drained quality of the pre-dawn, but the day-time world that replaces it in the following Scherzo is clownish and strangely pompous, a perfect aural recall of the back-stabbing and obsessiveness eagerness-to-please of *Zhdanovschina*. Sitting at the heart of all this is a figure who would shortly reappear in the Tenth Symphony, not quite the movement's protagonist, certainly not its still, but possibly its unquiet centre, a motto consisting of the notes D-E flat-C-B. In German notation, this spells out D-S-C-H, unmistakably the composer's own signature. This is the *yurodivy* at his most masked and ironic, but also inscribing a flagrant graffito.

The third movement is another emotional passacaglia, a fresh outpouring of emotion for the dead of the Terror and the war. It reappears in the closing movement but unexpectedly transformed. Shostakovich was about to embark on the finale when he was forced to make his recantation to the Composers' Union. The closing sequence, marked *Allegro con brio* as if in bright optimism, is characterised as a Burlesque and cast in two-note (Stalin), three-note (the People) and four-note (Shostakovich) cells, a grisly dance-of-death that sees the two individuals – composer and *Vozhd* – gradually give way to the mass. This time, though, there is a question-mark. Shostakovich's lifelong faith in the People seems to be at its lowest ebb.

Chapter Seven

Chapter Seven

The poorly disguised distaste with which America welcomed an ailing, nervous Shostakovich to the Waldorf-Astoria peace conference in 1949 was a perfect expression of free-world complacency. The journalists, writers and fellow-musicians who met Shostakovich could not possibly have known what he had suffered over the last dozen years. What they saw was a man who seemed to represent the polar opposite of liberal individualism and self-determination, a man for whom art was a form of ideological ventriloquism. How ironic that at home Shostakovich should have been condemned for the first and for failing to live up to the second.

Just as the wartime hero seemed to have feet of clay, the wartime ally was also undergoing a radical transformation in Western demonology. The Soviet Union, like America born in revolution, was now part of a vast Manichean drama, an alternative history. Some weeks before Shostakovich received his infamous phone call from Stalin, *Komsomolskaya Pravda* announced that Alesander Fyodorovich Mozhaiski had engineered the first heavier-than-air powered flight in 1884, a generation before the Wright brothers. Later in 1949 the Soviet Union demonstrated that it might not have been the first nation to explode an atomic bomb but that it was not far behind in what quickly became an apocalyptic technological and strategic contest that brought the world close to disaster.

The Terror years seemed to have come round again. There were fresh purges as Beria and Malenkov weeded out the last remnants of the Zhdanov circle, and new show-trials, which now extended to what was becoming known as the "Soviet bloc". Most notorious of them was the "confession" under torture of the Hungarian Cardinal Mindszenty who was found guilty of treason and other offences and sentenced to life imprisonment. It was only the first of many such trials in Eastern Europe. Thousands of Russian political prisoners coming to the end of their sentences were deemed not to have made sufficient restitution and were simply rearrested as "repeaters". There were revolts in the Gulag during 1950 and 1951, "objective" confirmation that the repression had been justified in the first place, and put down with brutal satisfaction.

The *déjà vu* effect was underlined by a return of the old Revolutionary gigantomania. In October 1948, the *Vozhd* had unveiled "The Great Stalinist Plan for Remaking Nature", a project to transform the Siberian climate permanently by planting huge forests. It was abandoned five years into its span when the Russian King Canute breathed his last. It did, however, provide Shostakovich with a subject which pleased even Khrennikov. On his return to the Soviet Union, he had been expected to produce a major work like the Fifth Symphony or possibly one of the abandoned Karl Marx- or Lenin-inspired works to redeem his reputation. Shostakovich's oratorio *Song of the Forests*, Op 81, was orthodox enough to win him a Stalin Prize and the much needed stipend of 100,000 roubles that came with it. He also wrote acceptable film music, like *The Fall of Berlin*, Op 82, but the real Shostakovich can be gleaned from the next opus number. Dedicated to the memory of his friend Pyotr Villiams, the Fourth String Quartet was the work of a man embittered, anxious, angry, fearful, all understandably so, but also stoically defiant and, as ever, utterly absorbed in the making of music.

His personal sorrows were far from over. One does not necessarily hear his distress in the main work that occupied him in 1950, but in private Shostakovich began to drink vodka in larger amounts, a habit that perhaps explains the odd mixture of neglect and almost smothering affection he displayed to Galina and Maxim. This morbid distortion of the paternal instinct became even more evident after Nina's death, when the children were essentially left in the care of a housekeeper but subject to maudlin displays of emotion when their father was around.

Shostakovich was awarded a *dacha* at Bolshevo as a reward for having taken part in the peace congress but he never seems to have settled there, preferring for a time being the Varzar appartments at Komarovo and increasingly a specially reserved cottage in the Union of Composers' House of Creativity at Repino. Indeed, in 1961 he handed back the Bolshevo house and bought a new one at Zhukovka, an odd gesture since he was entitled to fund the second purchase with the proceeds. The Shostakovich children eventually inherited Komarovo.

Despite the profound suspicion of the authorities, Shostakovich was again sent abroad as a delegate to further peace conferences, travelling to Warsaw in the spring of 1950 and to Berlin just before Christmas 1952. He also headed Soviet delegations to music festivals in East Germany, notably the Bach bicentenary celebrations in July 1950. Shostakovich had returned to playing by this time and on the same trip also performed in Berlin in a piano version of Bach's Concerto for Three Harpsichords. More important personally, though, was hearing Tatiana Nikolayeva playing Bach in Leipzig. Her pianism was an immediate inspiration to him and on returning home Shostakovich began work on his own Twenty-Four Preludes and Fugues, Op 87.

It is a very different work to the earlier Op 34 Preludes, which had been written as daily exercises while the wrangles over *Lady Macbeth of Mtsensk* continued. The later sequence has little of its predecessor's air of musing privacy and it is significant that though he did later make a recording, Shostakovich did not play the cycle in public. He did, however, have to present the work to his masters for their approval or constructive "criticism". He began work on the Preludes and Fugues in October 1950 and worked hard on the score at the Composers' Colony at Ruza, completing the work in February. In May he submitted to what had become a routine discipline, playing the work over two nights to a small audience of stone-faced Party officials at the Union of Composers. As he played, they scribbled on their notepads.

At the end of the performance, Shostakovich came forward – looking exhausted – to explain the work's genesis. His remarks were the now familiar mixture of self-denial, diffidence and defiance. He told the body that he had "always found it quite hard to compose, and therefore, so as to make it easier for me perhaps, I too have to practise this sort of scribbling". He explained that he had been influenced by Bach, and by the reassuring thought that even the master needed this kind of exercise to keep his technique honed. Nevertheless, the work seemed to write itself, and still seemed so fresh that he found it difficult to offer any personal judgement of it.

This amounts to an admission of formalism in the lower-case sense, or it may be that once again Shostakovich was throwing up neutral-coloured smoke to hide his real feelings. On Party instructions he was receiving home lessons in Marxist political economy at this time and was learning to dull their boredom with acts of exaggerated self-abasement: "I am a worm compared to His Excellency". The first listeners were unambiguous in their opinions. One Sergei Skrebkov, then a secretary at the Composers' Union, immediately pounced on the absence of any reflection of "Soviet reality" and damned the work as ugly. His old tormentor Zakharov, who had denounced all classical music at the infamous Zhdanov meeting and been rewarded with a secretarial position for his correct thinking, warned Shostakovich that he should not slip back into old mistakes.

There were defenders at the meetings, notably the composer Georgi Sviridov and the pianists Maria Yudina and Tatiana Nikolayeva. The latter premiered the work in Leningrad just before and again just after Christmas 1952, but it was Yudina who spoke up for the need to have music with "inner content" as well as music that simply reflected contemporary reality. She also defended the work's occasional moments of satire. What, in this world, could be wrong with that?

Surprisingly, one looks in vain for any deeply coded significance in the Twenty-Four Preludes and Fugues. Shostakovich told his first audience that he did not think of the piece as a unified cycle but a series of exercises and it is hard to avoid that impression. The middle and final fugues are magnificent, but there is a faintly academic air to the pieces, interspersed with claustrophobic melancholy, which suggests that Shostakovich really was trying to write his way out of a blocked or fallow period.

It may have worked. Within a year, Shostakovich had written a tough, muscular new string quartet, a piece that seems to allude in every movement to his own past but with a new defiance and perhaps with a sense that things were at last about to change. Its great sequel, the Tenth Symphony, would be one of his greatest and would emerge in that new – albeit chastened and still anxious – world that the quartet seems to promise. In the meantime, though, he continued to make a living as a performer, touring the Baltic republics and the Transcaucasus and writing the occasional rather routine score, including a cantata *The Sun Shines Over Our Motherland,* Op 90, again to words by one of the regime's most reliable poets Yevgeny Dolmatovsky, who had written the words for Shostakovich's entry for the wartime national anthem competition. The only other significant work of 1951 was *Ten Choral Poems on Revolutionary Texts,* Op 88, though he returned to more agreeable – even nostalgic – material at the beginning of the following year with the *Four Monologues on Verses by Pushkin,* Op 91.

There is a multiple irony in Maria Yudina's remark. For a time in 1952 it seemed that the regime agreed with her. In April *Pravda* announced that satire was dead in Russia and that the country needed a new Gogol to poke a little constructive fun at the "shortcomings" in Soviet society. Given that the socialist paradise was a matter of official *fiat,* and that the right-wing anarchist Gogol was not a name normally bandied about in the official press, this should have sounded warning bells. The very few Russian writers who took up the challenge were immediately arrested and charged with "unpatriotic libel". Boris Pasternak was in the final stages of *Dr Zhivago* but was probably by now so case-hardened – his mistress Olga Ivinskya had just been deported to the Gulag – that he would not have taken the bait. Those who did were mostly obscure and their work forgotten.

The *Pravda* editorial was a honey-trap. It would be another year before there were real signs of thaw. In November 1953, *Pravda* announced a more realistic attitude to Socialist Realism. In response, Khachaturian published a short article that called for modest freedom of expression for composers. The following month, the literary magazine *Novy Mir* published an essay called "On Sincerity in Literature" by Vladimir Pomerantsev which suggested that in future realism in fiction should be judged acccording to actual, empirical standards rather than abstract ideals. It looked as though a thaw might be coming. Like Pasternak, though, Shostakovich kept his thoughts to himself. He was wise to, for a year later *Novy Mir*'s editor was dismissed for having published the Pomerantsev article. The delay is significant, reflecting not so much immediate retribution for an ideological lapse, as a further brutal about-face. It was the falsest of springs.

A second audition of the Twenty-Four Preludes and Fugues had been called in the summer of 1952 by the Committee for the Arts and this time the work, so thoroughly calumniated mere months before, was praised to the skies. That effectively cleared it for public performance and Tatyana Nikolayeva set about learning the score. Her work with Shostakovich at this period yields a fascinating insight, that the composer had begun work on his Tenth Symphony long before the date normally assumed. It is clear from the whole course of Shostakovich's career that his major works – and the symphonies in particular – all had a long slow gestation and were often intermingled in his mind with smaller-scale works. The very fact that he was contemplating another symphonic work at all was a sign of some optimism, but something of that was already evident in the String Quartet No 5 in B flat, Op 95.

This remarkable piece was written in under a month, between September 7 and November 1 1952. Its predecessor had still not been publicly performed, and the stirrings of the Tenth Symphony must have been uppermost in his mind. Nevertheless, Shostakovich forged ahead with the work and it is one of his finest

A proud and devoted father, Shostakovich encouraged every aspect of Maxim's musical career. A music lesson photographed in Moscow in 1954

in the form. The opening seems innocuous enough but is soon packed with extraordinary dissonances and contentions between the violins and the other two strings. There are references to *Lady Macbeth of Mtsensk* (still possibly the work he most treasured) here and in the slow movement, and references, too, in bewildering profusion to the symphonies of the Terror and war years. The climax of the work is anything but unambiguously affirmative, but there is light and movement in the Fifth Quartet, a new, stronger and possibly shrewder creative identity. Underneath it all, but this time so utterly transformed that it is seldom commented upon, is the four-note D-S-C-H motto that was to become the almost obsessive signature of the Tenth Symphony.

ДМИТРИЙ ДМИТРИЕВИЧ ШОСТАКОВИЧ

When asked what that work was about by Solomon Volkov, Shostakovich said plainly that its subject was Stalin and Russia in the Stalin years. To some extent, this had been the subject of every major work for the last two decades, but with the Tenth that subject matter could come to the fore with new force and clarity, not least because by the time it was first heard The Greatest Genius Of All Centuries and All Nations was no longer around to hear it.

Between March 1953 and November 1955, three of the people who had made the greatest impact on Shostakovich left him and the world. The early months of 1955 saw the eventual premiere of *From Jewish Folk Poetry,* Op 79, which Shostakovich had suppressed during the time of institutionalised anti-Semitism. He also completed soundtrack music for *The Gadfly,* Op 97, a flowing Tchaikovskian score that has remained perhaps the best-loved of his occasional works. For the rest of the year, though, he composed little and spend much of his time at Komarova, nursing his 77 year old mother. Having survived a violent mugging twenty-one years before and the rigours of wartime Leningrad, Sofia Kokaoulina died on November 9.

If hers was an expected loss, that of Nina the year before had been shockingly sudden. A trained physicist, she had been working on cosmic radiation at a maximum security installation in Armenia when she fell ill and was discovered to have terminal cancer of the bowel. The couple had been living apart for some time – Nina was having an affair, or at least an intense emotional friendship, with her colleague Artem Alikhanian, while Shostakovich was involved with his brilliant composition student Galina Ustvolskaya – but when Shostakovich heard the news he immediately flew to be at her bedside. She died shortly afterwards and was brought back to Moscow for burial. It was under a cloud of grief that the widower played the piano part in *From Jewish Folk Poetry* at its première five weeks later.

It should have been a time of fresh optimism and renewed energy for Shostakovich. The greatest single obstacle to his life and happiness had been removed some time previously. In his final years Joseph Stalin grew increasingly paranoid. Plots against him—most of them imaginary—proliferated. He spent most of his last months behind the wire fences, booby-traps and mines that surrounded his dacha. After the 19th Congress in October 1952 he had re-organised the Party once again, preparing for yet another mass purge. The struggle for succession began, clandestinely and in an atmosphere of deep dread. On March 5 1953 Stalin slowly choked to death as the result of a cerebral haemorrhage, and apparently haunted by visions played out on his sickroom ceiling. He had lain unattended for some time, those around him too fearful to approach the soiled, stertorously breathing remains of the man who had been proclaimed the greatest and wisest ruler of all times but who they also knew to be one of history's most pitiless mass murderers. On the very same day, Sergei Prokofiev died in Moscow, and was denied his full obituary as ordinary Russians went into a bizarre spasm of grief. The killing did not end until Stalin was safely bricked up in the Kremlin Wall. Many in the hysterical crowds that gathered to file past his coffin were crushed by tanks. It was both a legacy and a dark prophecy.

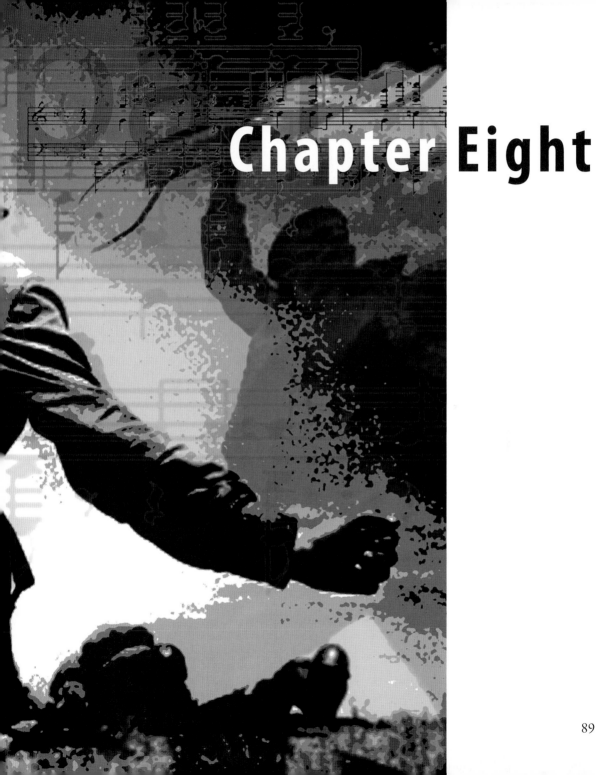

Chapter Eight

Chapter Eight

The Symphony No 10 in E minor, Op 93, is one of Shostakovich's very greatest works. In the wake of Stalin's death, he retreated once again to Komarova and resumed work on a score which, according to Tatiana Nikolayeva, had obsessed him for some time. The harsh lockstep that marched across earlier symphonies seems to have gone. Stalin's absence is audible. Instead the huge opening movement unfolds as a wheeling waltz in which three interlocking themes, largely built out of three-note cells, move in three-quarter time. In Shostakovich's numerology, this inescpably points to the Russian people, suddenly but ambiguously released from the tyrant's grip. As an aural representation of the coming Thaw, it is near perfect. It is also virtuosic symphonic writing. Soviet listeners chose to hear traditional folk material in its melodic content. Anyone listening now cannot help but be struck by its daring modernity.

And yet the Tenth Symphony is not free of shadows. The terrible weight of the past re-asserts itself in the middle of the movement. The ghost of Stalin can be heard yelling its familiar two-note figure, and the Scherzo which follows is almost entirely dominated by the Georgian *gopak* metre which had come to stand for the tyrant in Shostakovich's work. So far, so very similar to the implicit drama of previous symphonies, though never before had Shostakovich laid out his theme in quite such a complex manner. The Allegretto third movement is more mysterious, or is at least until the now familiar D-S-C-H motto comes to the fore, interspersed with horn clarions which some have traced back to Mahler. Implicit here is a certain retreat from history, an absorption in the self and in music of great inwardness. The movement also refers obliquely to a central motif in *Lady Macbeth of Mtsensk*, a treasured work which Shostakovich would shortly revise. There is a hint of warning, as if to say: Stalin may be gone; I may be moving from the spotlight; but things will go on as much as before, only secretly. Like all conscious Russians, Shostakovich must have been aware that to be relieved of Stalin only to fall into the bloodied hands of Lavrenti Beria – the former secret policeman was now locked in a power struggle with Georgi Malenkov and Vyacheslav Molotov – was a very ambiguous fate indeed.

There is a curious air of farewell about the Tenth Symphony. Given that his Fourth had still not been performed, Shostakovich may well have regarded it as a *de facto* ninth, since Beethoven an almost mystical number for a writer of symphonies. Mahler was haunted by it and did not live to see his Ninth Symphony performed. He also failed to complete his Tenth, which might help explain some of the Mahlerian references in Shostakovich's work. He himself was haunted by the possibility that he had nothing more to write, likening himself in one letter to Rossini who had written his last work at the age of forty and then lived on for his full biblical span without putting down another note.

The block that afflicted Shostakovich after the Tenth Symphony can be attributed to many things: to Nina's death; his mother's; to the inevitable rough handling the work received at the Composers' Union. Above all, though, it is a reflection of the enormous effort that went into the work. It is a masterpiece of compression, allusiveness and control. It also finishes with the only real and unambiguous apotheosis he had hitherto felt able to write. The second subject of the third movement and the great finale which celebrates – or more realistically looks forward to – the liberation of the Russian people are both liberally inscribed with the D-S-C-H motto, which sounds increasingly defiant and self-confident. It is not yet over, the Tenth Symphony seems to say, but there is a way through the darkness.

The Tenth Symphony was premiered under Mravinsky on December 17 1953. It is a mark of the uncertainty under which everyone had lived since the death of Stalin that there was no immediate or outright criticism, but it was determined that the work should be subject to proper scrutiny. A week later, Beria was executed (begging for his life according to one, universally enjoyed version, killed in a firefight according to the more likely one). The following March, the Tenth Symphony came before the Composers' Union. True to form, Khrennikov excoriated it. Ivan Dzherzhinsky, who Shostakovich had helped with his *Quiet Flows the Don*, was another of the attackers. The familiar consensus was that the work was individualistic and failed to reflect the realities of Soviet life. In a devastatingly simple and effective ploy – the *yurodivy* again – Shostakovich admitted that he'd made mistakes: the first movement was too long and the others disproportionately short... Significantly, he said nothing about its content.

The last three months of 1953 had seen a flurry of premières, the Fifth Quartet, then the Fourth, then the Tenth Symphony. The spring of 1954 saw little activity. The beginning of the year saw the first performance of the delightful Concertino for Two Pianos, Op 94, which was written for Maxim, who was studying at the Moscow Conservatoire and bent on a performing career. Shostakovich later wrote the Second Piano Concerto for the boy as well, but Maxim eventually settled on conducting as a career. Galya meanwhile seemed to have more of her mother's scientific genes and enrolled as a student of biology at Moscow University. The teenage children must have been alarmed by their father's depression, though they were by this time used to his absences and utter absorption in music; he and Maxim at least had that bond. What they thought when Shostakovich remarried just eighteen months after Nina's death isn't reliably recorded, but friends were appalled.

Margarita Kainova seems to have been a totally different personality to Shostakovich's vivacious and cultured first wife and the attraction seems to have been based entirely on her physical resemblance to Nina. They had met at the World Festival of Youth where Shostakovich was judging yet another "massed song" competition and Margarita was working for Komsomol. He engineered an introduction through his friend Lev Lebedinsky. It was an uneasy union, based on no apparent common interest, and in 1959 Shostakovich divorced Margarita, leaving Maxim to remove her from the Moscow flat.

If his private life was disastrous, his public career proceeded cautiously and in some respects rather strangely. Shostakovich continued with his film work and wrote music for Grigori Kozintsev's *Hamlet*. He had already cannibalised his *Hamlet* music from the 1932 production for Kozintsev's earlier *King Lear*. The two Shakespeare plays remained close to his heart. Almost the only other music written in 1954 was a *Festival Overture*, Op 96, to mark the 37th anniversary of the Bolshevik Revolution. While it is clear than air of tragedy would not be fitting in such a work, it is an extraordinary score in that it almost entirely lacks the mordant irony one expects to find in Shostakovich. More disturbingly, that same referential quality, full of quotes, allusions, secret codes and *mise-en-abîme* effects, seem to be entirely lacking even from a much more personal work, the Sixth String Quartet, which marked his return to canonical forms. They are also largely missing from the Eleventh Symphony, Shostakovich's first genuine critical success in the form since the Seventh.

Could it be that Shostakovich felt more in tune with the new regime? Or was he simply exhausted by the years of struggle and prepared to capitulate? Nikita Khrushchev had ousted Beria in July 1953, and restored the split in MGB (security and intelligence) and MVD (law enforcement) powers to create the *Komitet Gosudarstvennoy Bezopasnosti* which under its all too familiar initials remained the feared arm of Soviet internal and external security until the dramatic break-up of 1991. In February 1956, Khrushchev gave his famous "Secret Speech" to the 20th Congress of the Communist Party which for the first time expressed disquiet about Stalin's "errors". Any sign that Soviet society might be liberalising was tempered by brutal repressions elsewhere in the Soviet bloc. As the Central Committe signed an agreement eliminate the "cult of personality" – Khrushchev's ally Marshal Zhukov would shortly be a victim, though he was accused of having a "Buonaparte complex" – Russian tanks were crushing an uprising in Poland. That same October, the Hungarian rising was put down with overwhelming force by the Red Army. Some 30,000 died and throughout the West, loyal Popular Front Communists tearfully tore up their Party cards, while fellow-travellers quietly put away their Marxist-Leninist texts.

This was not a world in which a composer of Shostakovich's stamp could afford to be complacent. And yet the String Quartet No 6 in G major, Op 101, seems to inhabit a lighter, blander world than any of its predecessors. Again, it relies in its opening measures on a certain false simplicity that only gradually and subtly begins to reveal its satirical edge. The cheerful bucolic dances, with just a few belching interruptions from what still sounds like the old "Stalin" figure, are steadily revealed to be contrived, forced. Stalin may be gone, but in his place there comes a subtler propaganda. Instead of repression, self-repression; instead of rigorous Five Year Plans, photographs of smiling peasants and folk-dance troupes; while elsewhere armies still march, dissidents are still taken, the Gulag still functions. Evil recurs.

The idea of recurrence also figured strongly in the Symphony No 11 in G minor, Op 103. It is one of Shostakovich's largest scores, with forces that rival the Seventh, and perhaps for that reason has suffered a more lasting neglect in the West, criticised for bombast and shallowness. Its subtitle *The Year 1905* was dismissed by Michael Tippett as an "alibi" and Shostakovich himself made it clear that his symphony was about contemporary reality every bit as much as it related to that tragic failed people's revolution which had engaged his family's hopes so wholeheartedly just months before his conception. Listening to the Eleventh Symphony now, the impression is less of bombast than of disappointment, but all of it couched in what sounds like exaggerated optimism and passion. Though ostensibly inspired by Mussorgsky's populism, it exudes more of Tchaikovsky's doomed romanticism. The number three is everywhere, as always when Shostakovich wants to evoke the people, but here it is "the People" in abstract form. At the very moment the regime was proposing that all echelons of society – except the Politburo, needless to say – would benefit from some exposure to everyday labour, the people's composer seemed to have made an icon of them. Not surprisingly, the Eleventh Symphony was a resounding success.

Shostakovich seemed for the moment insulated from criticism. His 50th birthday on September 25 1956 was recognized with the Order of Lenin. Immediately after the 20th Congress discussions began as to whether the infamous 1948 decree on Formalism in music should be rescinded or at least re-evaluated. It was another two years before the Central Committee released an edict entitled "On the correction of errors". Its long title did not mention Shostakovich directly but the work of other, now obscure composers. Nevertheless, it formally ended Shostakovich's decade of critical ostracism. He was even asked to give a reply and vote of thanks to Khrushchev at a Kremlin reception for writers and intellectuals, a duty that would more naturally have fallen to Khrennikov. That put an official stamp on what was clearly a process of gradual rehabilitation, which had speeded up when Shostakovich was also asked to chair the jury of the internationally prestigious Tchaikovsky Competition. To have a non-person in such a role was unthinkable.

One thing soured his return to favour. The thought that his beloved *Lady Macbeth* might be revived was worth more to Shostakovich than a whole chest of medals and probably more than all the other works suppressed under the Zhdanov decree. In the spring of 1955 he responded to a request from the Leningrad Maly Opera and played a somewhat revised version of the opera to its directorate. Shostakovich was recommended to make direct application to Vyacheslav Molotov, then First Deputy Chairman of the Communist Party, that *Lady Macbeth* might be cleared for performance. There was a suspiciously long delay – during which time Shostakovich was partly distracted by preparations for the long-delayed première by David Oistrakh and Mravinsky of the First Violin Concerto – but an audition of the revised work was arranged for March 11 and 12 1956. The fact the Committee was prepared to come to Shostakovich's apartment at Mozhaiskoye Highway rather than summon him to the Union of Composers augured well. For his part, Shostakovich insisted that *Katerina Ismailova* (as the new version is known) should be sharply dissociated from the work which had prompted "Muddle Instead of Music". Unfortunately, his listeners reiterated the complaints of the infamous editorial almost word for word, condemned its content and the animalistic tone of the score. *Katerina Ismailova* was not cleared for performance for another five years, and even then was put in absurdly clandestine circumstances, disguised on posters as *The Barber of Seville*.

When the blow fell in 1956, expected but still shocking, Shostakovich simply straightened himself on the sofa where he had slumped after playing through the opera and thanked his listeners, fellow-musicians all, for their "criticisms".

Chapter Nine

Chapter Nine

Shostakovich's real response to the absurdities of the Zhdanov decree and its aftermath was probably hidden away in *Rayok*, the satirical cantata he based on Mussorgsky's own "peep-show", lampooning his contemporaries. There is some doubt about the exact dating and circumstances of the work, but the musicologist and RAPM founder Lev Lebedinsky – who claims to have written the libretto – dates it to the 2nd Congress of the Composers' Union, which took place in the spring of 1957. The apparent stimulus was the inability of a Central Committee official to pronounce the name Rimsky-Korsakov correctly, this from a man with direct responsibility for cultural matters. The official, Dmitri Shepilov, along with the musicologist Pavel Apostolov, Zakharov, Zhdanov and Stalin himself are quoted in the work, as is a Georgian folk song that was supposed to have been a favourite of the late *Vozhd*. Appended to the score is a mock-official rider "to help students" and portraying the work as dramatising the struggle between Realism and Formalism. Satire often relies on the conceit of the "found document" and Shostakovich's imaginary publisher (as if such a work could have been published!) claims to have discovered it buried in shit.

Rayok – or *Portrait Gallery* – was first performed in January 1989, in Washington, DC, and with Mstislav Rostropovich conducting. Like many of Shostakovich's friends, Rostropovich does not believe that a work of such open contempt for the regime could have been written any earlier than 1957, and certainly not in 1948 (the other suggested date) when Stalin was still alive and Shostakovich was living under the cloud of criticism and fear generated by the 1st Congress of the Composers' Union. Rostropovich does not seem to doubt, however, that the work, which is fairly meretricious in purely musical terms, was the work of Shostakovich alone and not an "exquisite corpse" passed among friends as a dangerously subversive parlour game and thus bearing the work of several hands.

There are questions about the exact authorship of *Katerina Ismailova* as well. Isak Glikman claimed to have had a hand in the revisions to Shostakovich's opera, and some observers have seen in its later, published version the hand of Irina Antonovna Supinskaya who worked on the literary side at the Sovietsky Kompozitor publishing house and who, in December 1962, four years after their first meeting, became Shostakovich's third wife. Their marriage came shortly after the premiere of Shostakovich's controversial Thirteenth Symphony, and from then

ДМИТРИЙ ДМИТРИЕВИЧ ШОСТАКОВИЧ

till the end, Irina was his loyal supporter and helpmeet.

Almost thirty years Shostakovich's junior (and thus almost his daughter's age), Irina was small, bespectacled, attractive rather than beautiful, and with a curious burr in her speech which led her to muddle *l* and *r* sounds. No one had quite understood the attraction of Margarita Khainova (to whom he was still married), other than her resemblance to Nina. With Irina, it was much more obvious. She was vibrant, clever, obviously devoted to "Mitya", and her history could only have moved his heart. Born in Leningrad, her father had been swept up in the Terror, while her grandparents died during the siege. Irina had been raised in one of the state orphanages - the Communist Party's version of magdalen houses–reserved for dissident families. In addition, as a seven year old, she had been been evacuated to Kuibyshev, where the Shostakovich children had spent the war and where the Seventh Symphony was first performed. Her only shortcoming was that she was married when she and Shostakovich first met.

Irina helped prepare the definitive version of *Katerina Ismailova* for publication, and also worked on the published text of *Moscow-Cheryomushki,* Op 105, a comic operetta written in 1958 about the new high-rise flats that Khrushchev was throwing up all over Moscow for workers and minor officials. Ironically, the building in 1961 of a new tower block to house the Composers' Union meant that Shostakovich (soon to be joined by Irina) moved into apartments in the old building, the very place where he had suffered his deepest personal and professional humiliations.

If he seemed happier and more youthful, the appearance was deceptive. The Shostakovich who visited the United States and Central America again in 1959 was no more vital and relaxed a man than the pale, nervous figure of the previous decade, but then he was travelling in company with the hated Khrennikov and was required to give cheerleading answers to questions about Russian music and Russian society. He spent that summer working on the Cello Concerto No 1 in E flat, Op 107, which was premiered in Leningrad on October 4, with its dedicatee Rostropovich as soloist and Mravinsky as conductor. In contrast to the work of previous years, it is alert, open writing, with a vividness of touch and a new confidence even in its satirical elements, as when the same Georgian folk song used in *Rayok* to make fun of Stalin is quoted again.

The concerto is also a work of notable simplicity, based on a single theme which then grows organically through both the solo and orchestral parts. In Rostropovich, the composer had found the perfect conduit for his work, an "instrumental" voice of genuinely democratic power. There was a further dimension to their relationship at this time. Shostakovich and Rostropovich had performed regularly on tour in the Soviet Union and in 1957 it was decided to record one of the staples of their repertoire, the joyous Cello Sonata from 1934, for the state recording label Melodiya. Unexpectedly, Shostakovich had difficulty executing some of the right hand chords and Rostropovich had to help him out. He had begun to suffer pain in that hand the previous year, but the problem continued to worsen and he was hospitalised for treatment in January 1960. His career as a performer was in jeopardy.

Shostakovich wrote a substantial amount of music in 1960, including one of his unquestioned masterpieces, but that crabbed, painful hand also inscribed a signature on one of the most controversial documents of Shostakovich's career, an application to join the Communist Party. As a purely personal decision, it seems mystifying, and was a shock to his friends. After years of stoical resistance, was Shostakovich capitulating? Some even claimed that he had been drunk when he signed a pre-filled form, and thus had no real hand in the "application". Given his record, before and since, of signing documents he had not read or could not possibly approve, it is not outside the realms of possibility. He had rather cravenly put his name to an official condemnation of novelist Alexander Solzhenitsyn and physicist Andrei Sakharov, one of the pioneers of the Soviet H-bomb. In context, the decision to apply is somewhat less strange. Khrushchev wanted to attract leading intellectuals to the Party, largely to counter an impression in the West that all Russian artists were automatically "dissident". There were limits to his toleration and they certainly did not stretch to Boris Pasternak who had been awarded the Nobel Prize for literature in 1958 but had been forced to renounce *Dr Zhivago* (and the laureateship) shortly before being expelled from the Writers' Union. For the last two years of his life – Pasternak died at the end of May 1960 – he was hounded mercilessly by the authorities.

Shostakovich, on the other hand, was increasingly seen as an establishment figure. He was invited to give composition masterclasses to post-graduate students at Leningrad Conservatoire, and would later be elected to the Supreme Soviet of the USSR, but in the meantime the condition of his election as chairman of the RSFSR Composers' Union was that he joined the Party. He was accepted as a candidate member in September 1960 – the immediate reward was that the Eighth Symphony was allowed back into the repertory – and received his full Party card the following autumn. But even this descended into farce. So nervous was Shostakovich of the step he was taking that he left Moscow for Leningrad shortly before the admission was to take place and took refuge with his sister, sending a sick note to apologise for his absence. He seems to have gone through a suicidal episode after making his application. Lebedinsky, an old Bolshevik who had long since lost faith in the Soviet system, remembers taking sleeping pills away from him.

These feelings suggest a context for the great works of 1960. Coming in order of completion between the Seventh and Eighth Quartets was a work for voice and piano, the openly dissident *Satires,* Op 109. This Shostakovich cautiously subtitled *Pictures of the Past,* though the Moscow audience demanded two full-length encores of the work when the composer and soprano Galina Vishnevskaya premiered the work in February 1961. The texts were taken from the work of poet and children's writer Sasha Cherny, the pen-name of A M Glikberg, who had left Russia after the Revolution and who died in France in 1932, ironically while fighting a fire. The wartime firefighter Shostakovich had read Cherny's poems while evacuated to Kuibyshev, but the stimulus to write something around them had to wait until anti-Semitism was no longer a plank of state policy – Cherny was a Jew – but also until he had found a voice as flexible and beautiful as Vishnevskaya's. Formerly a music-hall singer, the Bolshoi's leading soprano had made her name as Tosca and Violetta – doubtless Shostakovich heard her as Katerina Ismailova in his dreams; she later played the role in Mikhail Shapiro's 1966 film version – and was married to Rostropovich. The couple fell foul of the Soviet authorities when they harboured Aleksandr Solzhenitsyn in their summer house; they left the Soviet Union the year before Shostakovich's death and were stripped of citizenship four years later.

Shostakovich wrote other pieces for Vishnevskaya. The soprano part in the Fourteenth Symphony was inspired by her, and she was the composer's chosen interpreter for his orchestration of Mussorgsky's *Songs and Dances of Death* (also heard at the sensational February 1961 concert and orchestrated the following year) and the *Seven Romances on Poems of Aleksandr Blok*, Op 127, five years later. However, *Satires* should not be underestimated relative to these more prominent works. The piece – and reaction to it – both show that Shostakovich was still understood and more important understood himself to be playing a double game, conforming in outward particulars while still cocking a snook at Soviet society in the guise of a costume drama.

In contrast to *Satires,* the first of the 1960 string quartets is so personal a work that it scarcely seems fitted for public performance at all and were it not such a masterpiece of structural control it might well be allowed to sit apart from the official sequence of Shostakovich's chamber works. The String Quartet No 7 in F#, Op 108, is very short, just under twelve minutes in length, and consists of three connected movements. Its changes of mood – brisk, buoyant opening, slightly desolate middle section and dramatic, anxiety-ridden third movement before the opening subject returns in apotheosis – are easy enough to decode when one reads the work's superscription to the late Nina Vasilyevna. This is Shostakovich's musical farewell to his late wife. The opening is a wholly convincing sound-picture of the bright, combative woman remembered by friends. The movement's developing tensions are consistent with the volatile nature of the marriage. The middle movement hints at separation, interrupted abruptly by Nina's decline and Shostakovich's hectic flight to Yerevan to see her before she died. The return of the opening theme sees her spirit triumphant over death. There are other possible readings, and of course it is possible to read the work entirely as a triumphant exercise in form, but it would be perverse to ignore the autobiographical element and the emotion that attended it.

Its successor is also unmistakably autobiographical, and in some respects represents a companion piece. Shostakovich seemed to regard the Eighth Quartet as a memorial to himself, undertaken in a spirit somewhere between self-pity and defiance. He characterised its mood to Glikman as "pseudo-tragedy" – self-deprecation? the *yurodivy* speaking again? – and described how while composing it "my tears flowed as abundantly as urine after downing half a dozen beers". The tears came again when he played it through after returning home, though this time they were prompted not by the "pseudo-tragedy" but in admiration at his own wonderful unity of form.

Apart from the Fifth and Seventh Symphonies, none of Shostakovich's

works has been subject to such scrutiny as the String Quartet No 8 in C minor, Op 110. The reference to his arrival home confirms that the work was largely written in East Germany where in July 1960 Shostakovich visited Dresden, target of the notorious Allied firebombing of February 1945 in which at least 25,000 were killed. His ostensible purpose was to write soundtrack music for a film, *Five Days, Five Nights*. For all the vulgar diffidence of his comments, Shostakovich was clearly moved by the suffering the people and, in the burning of the city itself, by the destruction of one of the symbols of Baroque humanism. The Eighth Quartet bears the inscription "In memory of the victims of Fascism" and is often referred to as the "Dresden Quartet", particularly in Russia.

Good, and subtle, propaganda, for what one hears in the work when primed with that purely circumstantial title is a sound-picture of war, complete with droning glissandi to represent the sirens and great bursts of sound to suggest the brutal ordnance that set off Dresden's firestorm. It suited the Khrushchev regime very well that a rehabilitated "Formalist" should have contributed a work that so clearly expressed solidarity with the wartime suffering of an "ally" and that was so bracingly "realist" in approach. But is that really what the Eighth Quartet is about? The film music written in Dresden carries very little sign of strong emotion. Take away the programmatic title and superscription, and the Eighth Quartet turns into one of Shostakovich's most personal and self-referential works, a curiously wrought autobiographical monument. Writing to Glikman, Shostakovich suggested that the real title should be "Dedicated to the author of this quartet" and listed all the references contained in this "little miscellany".

The quartet begins with the now familiar D-S-C-H monogram but very soon quotes the First, Fifth, Eighth and Tenth Symphonies, the Piano Trio, the Cello Concerto and *Lady Macbeth*, all works with a profound resonance for their creator. In addition, it alludes to Wagner, the Funeral March from *Gotterdammerung* and the first movement of Tchaikovsky's *Pathetique* Symphony. What, he rhetorically asks in *Testimony*, do any of these have to do with Fascism? With the possible exception of the Wagner, one has to say: nothing. Unless, that is, one accepts the possibility (noted by Lebedinsky) that Shostakovich considered himself one of the victims of state fascism, and that the references back to the prison songs of *Lady Macbeth* and to the old revolutionary song "Tormented by Grievous Bondage" were a way of signifying that Shostakovich himself had lived in a state of virtual captivity. In that case the Eighth Quartet's public and private meanings precisely intersect.

When the new Party member decided to dedicate his Twelfth Symphony, written in the summer of 1961, to *The Year 1917,* it looked as though his capitulation was complete. The "Lenin Symphony" he had used as a smokescreen in 1938 looked like becoming an embarrassing reality, though it has been suggested that the original intention was to write a work that caricatured and satirised Lenin; an unthinkable heresy. Shostakovich could not overcome a visceral conviction that "Stalinism" was merely Leninism with a Georgian accent. He had always made it clear that Lenin, too, was a tyrant and that he despised the hagiographers who had turned him into an otherworldly spirit. That is alluded to in the strangely hymn-like melody which seems to identify Lenin in the Twelfth Symphony, but which constantly slips back into a more earthly register when confronted with the kind of material that always signals "the People" in Shostakovich's work. And there is a reference back to a very early work, something Shostakovich did ever more frequently in his last years, most notably in the Viola Sonata, Op 147, his last catalogued work, where he takes in the whole sweep of his career with a single reference. Here, it is more pointed, an allusion to the *Funeral March for the Victims of the Revolution*, where all of Shostakovich's ambivalence – hope soured by violence, liberty trampled by authority – is brought into play.

 The Twelfth Symphony is a curious work, not so much employing irony as utterly wrapped in it. Somewhat like the Eighth Quartet, it needs to be understood in a quite specific context. When the symphony was given its first British performance at the Edinburgh Festival in 1962, listeners were appalled by its sardonic tone. The irony had been inaudible at the première because the work was chosen to be played at the 22nd Congress of the Soviet Communist Party, just a few weeks before Shostakovich was accorded full Party membership. This was the setting for Khrushchev's second attack on Stalin, which led to the *Vozhd's* remains being removed from their place of pilgrimage in Red Square. In future, only Lenin was to be the object of such veneration. Shostakovich, who had suffered under Stalin, had grasped the *Zeitgeist* by writing his Lenin symphony (even if it was no such thing). Once again, the self-serving logic seemed to have come up with an acceptable equation of politics and creativity. Once again, fresh disproof was just around the corner.

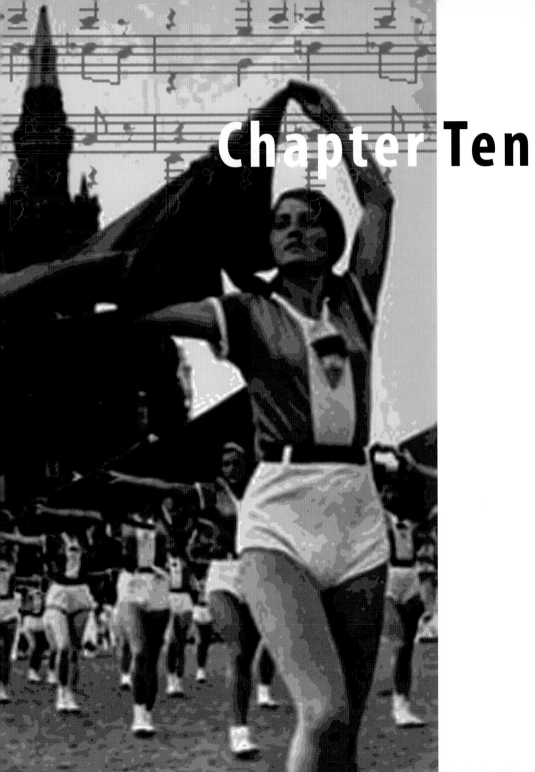

Chapter Ten

Chapter Ten

Twelve weeks after the première of the Twelfth Symphony – to a spectrum of reactions that would eventually run from official approval to public indifference at home and outright hostility abroad – an earlier, more cherished work was eventually brought out into the light. On the last but one day of 1961 Kirill Kondrashin – who Shostakovich had come to trust as much as Mravinsky – gave the downbeat that began the belated first performance of Shostakovich's Symphony No 4 in C minor, Op 43, which had been written, rehearsed and abandoned half a lifetime earlier. Along with *Lady Macbeth of Mtsensk* it is one of the composer's masterpieces. It may be that the work's revival was a sop to Shostakovich, in return for the relatively conformist Twelfth Symphony. There was perhaps a growing coolness between Shostakovich and Mravinsky, who had always been his conductor of choice, but who had a lofty manner and a mandarin disregard for others. Rostropovich found him arrogant and remote. It seems that under the influence of his wife, Mravinsky had declined to conduct the Thirteenth Symphony, fearing its content. In Kondrashin, Shostakovich had found not just a substitute, but a conductor passionately committed to the music, and as the composer wrote it.

The problem with the Fourth Symphony was finding the music. The score had been lost during the war, possibly burnt to heat the Leningrad apartment during the siege. Some orchestral parts were discovered in the city, though, and Shostakovich undertook to examine them and to create a piano reduction. It was assumed, not least by Shostakovich himself, that he would have to make substantial revisions but he told Kondrashin that he was happy with the work as it stood and the Fourth Symphony was put into rehearsal, without this time the problem of a frightened and obstructive conductor.

The reaction of one listener is telling. Shostakovich had met the scientist Flora Litvinova and her husband Mikhail Litvinov while evacuated to Kuibyshev. She was one of the old friends Shostakovich invited to the premiere. Litvinova was stunned and somewhat discomfited. "Why do Dmitri Dmitryevich's later works lack those qualities of impetuosity, dynamic drive, contrasts of rhythm and colour, tenderness and spikiness?" It was not an entirely rhetorical question, for Litvinova goes on to blame the 'historic' Decree which warped the living spirit in him".

Warped, but not broken. The revival of the Fourth Symphony and the evergreen hope of seeing *Katerina Ismailova* staged again seemed to light new fires in Shostakovich. His creative energies and reputation had both oscillated wildly since the Terror years, but rarely in synchronisation. Having won official approval with a relatively weak symphonic work, it now seemed inevitable that he would again face criticism for a great one.

The Soviet literary scene had changed even more dramatically than music during the thaw years. In 1962 and on the advice of Alexander Tvardovsky (who had been restored to his position as editor of *Novy Mir* during the second thaw) Khrushchev personally authorised the publication in the magazine of Solzhenitsyn's *One Day in the Life of Ivan Denisovich,* which became an international success in translation. Solzhenitsyn, though, was nearly 50 and with clear memories of the Terror, which coloured his later actions and statements. By the turn of the 1960s a new generation of writers had come forward with no such memories and with relatively high expectations of creative freedom, and would feel the backlash keenly.

One of them was the poet Yevgeny Yevtushenko, still not 30 years of age in 1962 but already much admired. In September 1961, his long poem "Babi Yar", which told of the Nazi massacre of 70,000 Ukrainian Jews at a ravine outside the city of Kiev in September 1941, was published in *Literaturnaya Gazeta.* Shostakovich read it shortly after the premiere of the Twelfth Symphony, still smarting from what he and friends considered to be a deeply compromised work. Yevtushenko had already emerged as the bellwether of youthful, intelligent dissidence, so Shostakovich telephoned him to suggest that he might make a setting of "Babi Yar". It was a huge vote of confidence for a young writer, and Yevtushenko enthusiastically accepted, providing Shostakovich with other texts and, ultimately, with a specially written poem.

It is usually said that Shostakovich initially intended to write a cantata based on "Babi Yar", but there is evidence that he saw in the work the potential to neutralise the disappointment of his Twelfth Symphony, and to reverse his old suspicion of Proletkult song-symphonies and verbal apotheoses by including a vocal part for only the second time in his symphonic career to date. The (misleading) conception of "Babi Yar" is that it only concerns the massacre. That is true of the first movement only. In subsequent movements, "Humour", "In The Shop", "Fears", and "A Career" Shostakovich and Yevtushenko dealt with wider issues, and not least the atmosphere that pervaded Russia during the pre-war Terror and the cynicism of authority. It seemed impossible that such a work could avoid controversy, even in an atmosphere of thaw.

Nothing complicated the censorship situation in Russia more than the immediate success of Solzhenitsyn's short novel. Widely admired and recognised as an officially sanctioned memoir of the bad old days, it let loose a flood of bottom-drawer manuscripts, journals and thinly disguised autobiographical fictions that immediately put Khrushchev's tentative moratorium on censorship into reverse. In December 1962, the leader visited an exhibition called "Thirty Years of Moscow Art" and launched an astonishing attack on contemporary culture, calling many of the artists represented in the show "pederasts", by which it is assumed he meant "masturbators". An even more thoroughgoing vulgarian than Stalin, and surrounded by philistine advisers, Khrushchev did not seem to understand what was meant by "abstraction" in art, using the word as an insult for anything he disliked. Shortly afterwards and despite the cachet of having his poem "The Heirs of Stalin" published in *Pravda*, Yevtushenko was attacked by one of Khrushchev's henchmen at a Kremlin reception for writers. Former *Izvestia* editor and recent head of agitprop and propaganda at the Central Committee, Leonid Ilyichyov objected to the implication in "Babi Yar" that only Jews, and not countless thousands of Slavs, and had died in the Nazi Holocaust. Soviet anti-Semitism reared its head again. Though later he submitted to pressure and reworked the poem, bringing down on his head the wrath of liberal intellectuals, Yevtushenko on this occasion bravely stood up to Khrushchev himself, even after the leader had growled an old country proverb about the grave curing cripples, a plain reference to the feeling that the best way of dealing with those warped by dissidence was simply to liquidate them. More alarming for Shostakovich, Ilyichyov expressed disgust that such nonsense as "Babi Yar" had been set to music. The regime had cleared the way to suppress the Thirteenth Symphony, then in rehearsal under Kondrashin.

Shostakovich had begun work on the score in June, after a short period in hospital. He finished the symphony in August, shortly before leaving for the Edinburgh Festival. It was clear on his return that there would be problems with the work, but it was decided to proceed with rehearsals, even after the first choice as bass soloist was ruled out and his replacement conveniently called away to sing a role for the Bolshoi. Perhaps stiffened by the renewed international fame the visit to Edinburgh had brought him, Shostakovich and his circle seemed bent on confrontation.

Once again, as he had with the First Violin Concerto and other works of 1948, Shostakovich seemed to identify strongly with the Jews. One of the passages later revised by Yevtushenko begins "I feel I am a Jew" and expresses an imaginative empathy with Christ on the Cross, an astonishing projection for Shostakovich, a lifelong atheist, to make. Once again, in seeming to write about other subjects and other times, he created an excoriating portrait of his own country and in the present tense. Though inevitably much of the emphasis surrounding the Thirteenth Symphony was and remains directed to its text, the musical language and codes are immediately familiar. Power is represented by thudding two-note *fortes*, the People by threes. There is ample quotation from earlier work, significantly from the Sixth Quartet, and yet the unities of the score seem forced in comparison with the recently revived Fourth Symphony. The work's unity comes very largely from Yevtushenko rather than Shostakovich.

On December 18 1962, it was greeted with wild acclaim in Moscow, though the official boxes remained conspicuously empty as Party officials stayed away to write their reports and reactions without the awkward prejudice of having actually heard the piece. It seemed to a sophisticated audience that Shostakovich had put aside his temporising and written passionately from the heart. Again, this was largely confirmed by Yevtushenko's writing. The association with a hot-blooded young writer raised the composer's credit, but it also served to disguise the sombre nature of the writing. Shostakovich's unadorned later style and aura of blank fatalism – tragedy is no longer the right word – can be traced to the fustian scoring of "In The Shop", where he portrays a world of shortages, queues, tasteless greyness.

For the moment, though, this was not of outward concern to the composer, who seemed to ride out the ensuing storm with Yevtushenko as his human shield. He had, in any case, other things to look forward to, marriage to Irina, and, in late December and January, the long-awaited revival of *Lady Macbeth*/*Katerina Ismailova.*

Though Shostakovich's music is all very much of a piece and difficult to divide up stylistically, the Thirteenth Symphony ushered in what was unmistakably a "late period", marked by slow, spacious music, punctuated by silences, but also with sharp percussion (which was probably the result of reworking the clangorous Fourth Symphony) and characterised by what in any other composer might be described as spirituality, if not religiosity. The tolling of church bells in the Thirteenth Symphony strikes an unexpected note. Flora Litvinova's comment about the preceding symphony is perhaps best treated as description, rather than criticism. Much of the nervous vitality of Shostakovich's music had disappeared. Some attribute this to ill health, and particularly to the problem with his right hand. Others have assumed that it is, simply and understandably, a reaction to the rigours and anxieties of the preceding thirty years, a chastening experience even for a less determined and stoical man.

Listening to the works of the final period, one hears a steadily deepening absorption in sound itself. The music becomes less linear, more meditative, and at times almost sculptural in its stillness. Shostakovich never approaches the massive sustains and repetitions of his pupil Galina Ustvolskaya, whose intensely spiritual, almost static "symphonies" for small instrumental groups were effectively banned. A whole generation of composers influenced by Shostakovich was emerging. Born in 1934, Alfred Schnittke had taken up the challenge of Shostakovich's implicit polystylistics and was embarked on a body of work that would recapture something of the master's sardonic energy. His earliest works, the Violin Concerto of 1958 and the oratorio *Nagasaki,* show little sign of a direct debt, though the later *concerti grossi,* postmodernist works written in a deliberately archaic form, are Shostakovich's most obvious progeny in Russian music, albeit written in the West. Rodion Shchedrin, who succeeded Shostakovich as president of the Union of Composers in 1973, defined himself as "post-avant-garde" and spent the early part of his career shrewdly brokering a safe establishment position with works like the 1951 piano piece *Festivity on a Collective Farm* and the much later *Solemn Overture* for the 60th anniversary of the USSR while at the same time using his official positions to camouflage an experimental cosmopolitanism.

Shostakovich had learned to perform the same creative sleight-of-hand with far greater subtlety. In the spring of 1964, having met the revered novelist Mikhail Sholokhov, he announced that he would be writing an opera based on Sholokhov's *And Quiet Flows the Don.* Once again, as the choice of subject perhaps confirms – he would have thought back wryly to Drzhezinsky's opera of thirty years before – this was an elaborate charade to distract attention from the work that really occupied him, the forcefully dissonant Ninth and Tenth Quartets.

These were both completed in 1964, a busy year for Shostakovich and for

Shostakovich acknowledges the applause at the Moscow Conservatory's gala evening celebrating his 60th birthday in 1966

Russia. After the severe food shortages of the previous year, it seemed unlikely that Khrushchev would hang on to power. His deposition in October in favour of the hard-liner Leonid Brezhnev would have far-reaching implications for artists and intellectuals. For the moment, though, Brezhnev and his second in command Alexei Kosygin were happy to promote the illusion that a new thaw had begun. Partly because of this, Shostakovich was able to maintain his carefully adjusted distance from the regime. There was no sign of any interruption in the flow of work. He spent much of December and January in the artists' colony at Repino, writing film music for Grigori Kozintsev's film of *Hamlet*. His Op 116 betrays no discernible sign of borrowing from previous *Hamlet*s. The music is absolutely integral to the film, but also stands alone strongly, full of the intense – "virulent" was the word Kozintsev

Дмитрий Дмитриевич Шостакович

preferred – philosophical quiddity that marked both subject and composer.

In February, the second Gorky Festival was devoted entirely to Shostakovich's music, a unique retrospective at the time, when music festivals were rare, and almost unknown in Russia. Shostakovich had sent the orchestral manuscript of *Songs of Love and Death* to its organiser Rostropovich for the previous festival, but the return accolade was no mere pleasantry, but recognition that Shostakovich was now not only the Soviet Union's greatest living composer – the return of Stravinsky for a visit in 1962 did not change that – but also relatively "safe". Shostakovich was, of course, deeply ambivalent towards his exiled countryman. He kept a photograph on his desk and loved Stravinsky's music, while apparently loathing his ideas and carelessly-worn cosmopolitanism. He seems to have avoided the encounter Stravinsky sought from the moment he arrived back on Russian soil. When he could no longer escape the inevitable, he seemed as nervous and unprepossessing as ever, though perhaps there is another explanation. Shostakovich could never take a compliment with ease. Nothing would reduce him to a chain-smoking, nail-chewing wreck quicker than flattery and Stravinsky now combined Russian passion with American ease of manner.

If 1964 was to be Shostakovich's last year of virtually full health, he used it productively and with a final flurry of his old obsessions. A cantata *The Execution of Stepan Razin,* Op 119, based on Yevtushenko's poem "The Bratsk Hydro-Electric Station", has all the familiar coding of two against three, authority against people. The same figures appear again, with a later version of the "betrayal" motif from *Lady Macbeth,* in the String Quartet No 9 in E flat, Op 117. It seems to be a transitional work, difficult to distinguish in its faster and more biting passages from any one of a number of previous quartets, but there is also a new quality in the music that suggests history has been transcended. The "*Muss es sein?/Es muss sein!*" questions and answers which became part of the language of string quartet writing with Beethoven's late masterpieces no longer refer to earthly or quotidian issues but to the large questions of being and non-being, fate and mortality. Shostakovich burned the first draft in his stove, something he had done before, in 1926, but a potent gesture that gives the lie to any suggestion the work was merely routine and academic, without the deep personal drama of its predecessor.

The String Quartet No 10 in A flat, Op 118, seems to compress much of the span of Shostakovich's composing career into its modest length. More conventional in structure to the Ninth, it follows the familiar pattern of quietly untroubled opening cut across by a mordant scherzo, followed by a mourning passacaglia, followed by ambiguous resolution. The only difference is that the final three notes sound very much like someone signing off. The two quartets were premiered together in November 1964. A few weeks later, in the dying days of the year, *The Execution of Stepan Razin* was performed in Moscow. The new year would mark the start of Shostakovich's final decade. He would write two more symphonies, a second Violin Concerto, five more string quartets (he had hoped to write 24, never repeating a key), and two instrumental masterpieces, one of which would only echo from beyond the grave.

Последний тост

Я пью за разоренный дом,
За злую жизнь мою,
За одиночество вдвоем,
И за тебя я пью, —
За ложь меня предавших губ,
За мертвый холод глаз,
За то, что мир жесток и груб,
За то, что Бог не спас.

Chapter Eleven

Chapter Eleven

Shostakovich wrote his final work, the Viola Sonata, Op 147, while convalescing from the latest onslaught of illness in the summer of 1975. He worked as usual at Repino. Shostakovich had always hated being asked what his "last" work was, when questioners meant his "latest", but the Viola Sonata was a clear-headed and philosophically robust farewell to composition, with an unambiguous nod to Beethoven in the magnificent slow finale. The composer's instructions to the work's dedicatee and first performer Fyodor Druzhinin was that it should sound not morbid or elegiac, but "bright, bright and clear".

Shostakovich's last decade was lived in the deepening shadow of ill-health. He had never been robust. The privations of the Civil War years had led to tuberculosis and throughout his life Shostakovich suffered from psychosomatic illnesses as he converted stress and anxiety into physical symptoms. As he approached his 60th birthday, however, his constitution seemed to be breaking down irretrievably. The problem with his hand was eventually diagnosed as poliomyelitis and Shostakovich joked wryly about an ailment still commonly described as "infantile paralysis". The affliction had caused him to fall down on several occasions, notably at Maxim's wedding, where he had broken his left leg. A few years later, he broke the other in a car accident while on holiday in Byelorussia, and limped visibly for the remainder of his days.

A heavy smoker and drinker, he began to suffer heart problems as well and was treated in a sanatorium in early 1965 for ischaemia and cardiac occlusion, as well as neurological problems associated with his polio. The following year, he spent some time convalescing at a sanatorium in the Crimea, where 42 years earlier he had met his first fiancée Tanya Glivenko. Worse was to follow. Four months short of his 60th birthday, he suffered a severe heart attack and spent the next six weeks at an institution outside Leningrad, in the very same rooms where – another grim physical coincidence in his life – one Andrei Zhdanov had once undergone drying-out treatment.

He was hospitalised again during 1969 and 1970, receiving neurological and cardiological treatment. In September 1971, during rehearsals for his last symphony, there was another significant heart attack. A year later, renal colic and lung cancer were diagnosed and Shostakovich underwent an intensive course of cobalt radiotherapy which failed to arrest the tumours. News of his illness was kept within the family.

112

Pain and debility did not seem to change his personality. Always nervous, his face a life's map of tics and twitches, he remained as physically restless and ill-at-ease in unfamiliar company as he had been as a young man. His opinions could be harsh and intolerant, and he often affected to forget personal details about people he had known for many years. He could be laconic and remote, almost pathologically shy. Close friends, though, found him warm, dryly funny and with a unstaunchable energy that when engaged seem to lift the years away. They recall the endless games of patience – latterly preferred to the excitement of poker – and Shostakovich's touching habit of noting down football scores in his newspapers as they were announced on radio.

Shostakovich also proved himself capable of making new friendships, even when the language barrier thwarted intimacy. In 1959 he met Benjamin Britten in London, when they were seated together at the Royal Festival Hall to hear Rostropovich play the First Cello Concerto. Music was their common language and though temperamentally Britten was very different, his music had much in common with Shostakovich's. Three years later, Rostropovich played Britten's

A rarely photographed smile. Shostakovich is amused in the company of Benjamin Britten and Peter Pears

Cello Symphony in Moscow and over the next few years, Britten and his partner Peter Pears saw a good deal of Shostakovich, spending a happy new year at Zhukova at the beginning of 1967 and on subsequent occasions. In turn, Shostakovich spent part of the summer of 1972 at Britten's home in Aldeburgh, where he began writing his Fourteenth Quartet. His horizons remained wide. In 1973, after receiving radiation therapy he was well enough to travel once again to the United States and to Britain. He had even made unexpected use of some serialist elements (then a virtual orthodoxy in the West) in the Twelfth Quartet, though they remain entirely consistent with its D flat tonality. Having remained faithful to his own vision for more than forty years he was not ready to do what Stravinsky had done in his late, serialist period, and surrender to cosmopolitanism or to a musical language drawn from any other than the classical well.

Stoical about most of his physical problems, there was one that disturbed him more than any. There was some relief from the problems in his right hand, but as it improved Shostakovich began to feel that his musical imagination was drying up. Though frequently in his life forced to accept that silence was the safer option, Shostakovich had never before suffered creative block. It is not an affliction normally associated with age. Unlike other fields of intellectual activity – mathematics most notably – a composer's powers do not seem to diminish with age and 20th century music was full of opsimaths – among them Elliott Carter and Michael Tippett – who seemed to work with ever greater fluency as they aged, even if they had to contend with unavoidable physical infirmities. One of these troubled Shostakovich deeply. Always myopic, he also began to lose his sight, making work on large scores increasingly difficult. He must have returned to *King Lear* again – thirty years on from his first approach to the play, the 1970 Op 137 is soundtrack music for Kozintsev's film version – with a tremor of wry recognition. It may well have seemed time to hand over his position at the head of Russian music to younger and fitter composers. He did stand down as first secretary of the RSFSR Union of Composers in April 1968. The political and cultural stagnation that had set in during Brezhnev's regime, only swept away more than a decade after Shostakovich's death, by the winds of *glasnost* and *perestroika* caused many even among the younger generation to wonder if the game was any longer worth the candle. The Stalinist years had been terrible and terrifying, but there is more energy in fear than in blank indifference and incomprehension. The great paradox of totalitarian regimes is that they take art and artists seriously and refuse to treat them as decorative appurtenances.

The music of Shostakovich's last decade has little of the power and vitality of his great works. It is less paradoxical, less obviously encrypted, and to some degree more emotionally open. Some of it, like the Fifteenth Quartet and the Viola Sonata, derives some of its resonance from an association with the deathbed. Some of it, like the late romances and the Michelangelo suite, are touched by a gentleness and philosophical calm that are new to his work. And yet, the great continuities remain. The organising principles of the late works are identical to those of the promising young student who presented his First Symphony as proof to his teachers that he could compose. Shostakovich's son-in-law, the film-make Yevgeny Chudovsky, who married Galina in 1959, remembers a conversation in which Maxim asked his father why he didn't simply pay someone to copy out orchestral part. Shostakovich replied, "Everyone should do his own work from beginning to end".

On May 28 1966, Shostakovich made his last significant appearance as a pianist, playing in a concert devoted to his work that included the premiere of *Five Romances on Texts from 'Krokodil'*, Op 134 (an innocuous set of songs based on the state-sponsored satirical magazine) as well as the more ironic, and not at all elegiac, *Preface to My Collected Works and a Short Reflection Upon This Preface*, Op 123. Despite working with Galina Vishnevskaya (who sang the *Krokodil* romances with Yevgeny Nesterenko) Shostakovich was crippled with nerves and the very next night suffered his heart attack.

It was perhaps a propitious time to be in convalescence. The wheel of Soviet favour and disfavour had made another creaking turn. Khrushchev had been discredited and unpersoned and there were moves afoot to rehabilitate the reputation of Joseph Stalin. In the field of literature repression had returned. Mikhail Sholokhov, with whom Shostakovich was supposed to have collaborated on *The Quiet Don*, publicly called for the death penalty for the dissident writers Yuri Daniel and Andrei Sinyavsky. They were sentenced to seven years hard labour instead but it became clear that with the accession of Leonid Brezhnev and a return to hard-line Stalinism freedom of speech was effectively in abeyance. *Samizdat* – or clandestine – publication became the norm. In early March 1966, the beloved Anna Akhmatova, perhaps the most potent symbol of Russian literature through the Revolution and Terror years and in that respect Shostakovich's poetic twin, died at Komarovo, haunted by the returning spectre of the man who had sent her son to the Gulag and made her sell her artistic soul in a fruitless bid to get him back.

Shostakovich had his own tried and tested method for dealing with the vagaries of politics. His String Quartet No 11 in F minor, Op 122, was written at Repino in January 1966, shortly before the satirical *Preface*. They have the same slightly skittish quality overlying a darker vision, much like the Fool's clowning in *King Lear*. In 1964, Shostakovich told a *Pravda* interview that his Ninth Quartet was concerned with childhood and "toys", but it seems that the Eleventh is closer to that playful spirit, or would be were it not for the darker strains that throb underneath the innocent – or *faux*-innocent – surface.

The same bare simplicity also surfaces in the Cello Concerto No 2 in G, Op 126, completed while convalescing in the Crimea. Here, though, it is woven into an altogether more complex structure which in the inverse ratio that applies to instrumentation and orchestration makes the work seem sparser still. Written again for Rostropovich, it should have been conducted by Mravinsky, to whom Shostakovich still felt some loyalty. Inexplicably, though, Mravinsky refused, claiming that he did not have enough time to learn the score. It was premiered under Yevgeny Svetlanov on Shostakovich's 60th birthday, September 25 1966, on which occasion he was awarded the Order of Lenin and made a Hero of Socialist Labour.

Once again, Shostakovich was less excited by the medals than by the release of the film version of *Katerina Ismailova*, whose familiar motifs now seemed to haunt his work, as if his entire musical history were somehow embedded in that great work's narrative of cultural paucity, betrayal, defiance, violence and imprisonment.

While convalescing, Shostakovich read poetry, always a solace but now an important spark to musical inspiration. Having avoided using texts for much of his career – the written word lacks the kind of ambiguity and covert protest that can be hidden away in instrumental scores – Shostakovich now seemed committed to text-setting. Forming a companion piece to the other stark, almost monolinear works of 1966 is the cycle *Seven Romances on Verses by Alexander Blok*, Op 127, for soprano and piano trio. Its simplicity is partly explained by his physical condition. Shostakovich wrote the work for Vishnevskaya, Rostropovich and David Oistrakh but hoped to be able to play the piano part himself. It is an intensely personal piece, beginning with a hymn to his native city and concluding with a strong assertion of the restorative power of music; Shostakovich felt that setting these resonant texts – particularly "Ophelia's Song", another *Hamlet* reference – and working with close and symphathetic friends allowed him to overcome a deepening creative block. During the same period of recuperation, he also chose the text for what became his Fourteenth Symphony.

History still intruded, however. The new repressions introduced by the Brezhnev regime applied mainly to writers and the new weapon was psychiatry. Dissidence was officially considered a form of mental illness and treated with a range of therapies ranging from electro-convulsive shocks and large doses of insulin to simpler and older remedies such as wrapping "patients" in freezing wet towels. Shostakovich became an important signatory to various petitions and open letters to the authorities, pleading for a restored freedom of expression. He took up the case of Alexander Solzhenitsyn, and did as the Rostropoviches had done and offered the novelist refuge at his dacha. It was a temporary alliance, because Solzhenitsyn objected to Shostakovich's militant atheism, and later broke with him completely.

Nevertheless, something of the "Jewish" solidarity of its predecessor emerges again in the Violin Concerto No 2 in C # minor, Op 129, the first major orchestral work written after the "block". Obviously disturbed by a new wave of censorship and repression, Shostakovich sets the solo violin's plangent lament, once again owing its basic material to *Lady Macbeth,* against an equally familiar two-note figure, transformed but still reminiscent of the "Stalin" motto of earlier works. What is different now is that "the People" seem to have less part to play, even as an abstraction. It is as if Shostakovich now sees the essential struggle as between authority and isolated individuals like himself. It may even be that the betrayal the work implies actually involves the people, too craven and hesitant to rise up and assert their freedom. The Second Violin Concerto is a complex work, troubling and magnificent by turns, majestic in parts but constantly interrupted by a kind of violent vulgarity.

The premières of the concerto (with Oistrakh again as soloist) and the Blok settings were played out against stirrings of dissent within the Soviet bloc. The

"Prague Spring" was just around the corner, but while its brutal repression certainly sparked a passionate response from Shostakovich, for the moment he was either too case-hardened or too involved in private concerns to reflect it directly in his music. For more than thirty years, the Beethoven Quartet had been the leading chamber ensemble in Russia and had given the first performances of all his string quartets except the first and last. Their interpretations of the late quartets only served to underline Shostakovich's growing identification with Beethoven himself, an association made explicit at the end of the Viola Sonata, but unmissable in other works of the last years. He had been deeply troubled when in 1965, the group's second violinist Vasili Shirinsky died suddenly. The "Beethovens" had lost their original violist the year before, when Vadim Borisovsky retired, to be placed by Fyodor Druzhinin. The Eleventh Quartet was dedicated *in memoriam* to Shirinsky and Shostakovich then wrote his next three quartets for the other original members: the Twelfth, with its unexpected serialist elements, was written for first violinist Dmitri Tsyganov, the Thirteenth for Borisovsky and the Fourteenth for Shirinsky's cellist brother Sergei, who died during rehearsals of the Fifteenth and final quartet, just months before Shostakovich's own death. It was Druzhinin who gave the posthumous premiere of the Viola Sonata.

These men were as close and important to Shostakovich as Vishnevskaya, Rostropovich and Oistrakh had become, trusted allies and friends who showed an almost telepathic understanding of the composer's needs, even if he sometimes had to give harsh criticism for mis-readings; for Shostakovich, unlike the great Rubinstein, the music as written was more important than "intepretation". In January 1969, Oistrakh gave the first performance of the Violin Sonata, Op 134, a work which, written against the bloody unravelling of the Czech experiment, rumbles with hidden griefs and anger.

That same month, Shostakovich was again in hospital, but while convalescing began work on the Symphony No 14, Op 135. In form, it is radically different from all his other symphonies. Indeed, Shostakovich seemed to think it might not be so numbered at all, but could not be classified as an oratorio because it was scored simply for a soprano and a bass voice, with just strings and percussion. Shostakovich had been inspired to write it by his earlier work on Mussorgsky's *Songs and Dances of Death*, but the themes of mortality and the people had been sharply quickened by recent events in Czechoslovakia. The Fourteenth stands somewhat apart from the run of Shostakovich symphonies, but it is a profound and powerful experience, blackly pessimistic and almost nihilistic in its *De profundis* section.

The authorities were well aware of its potentially subversive content and did all that they could to thwart public performance, short of an outright ban. Shostakovich was in haste to hear what he again believed might be his last, rather than latest, work and agreed to an effectively private performance for invited guests in a recital room at Moscow Conservatoire. He had decided to forgo using Vishnevskaya for the moment, since touring responsibilities had left her without sufficient time to learn the part. She sat in the audience, as did Solzhenitsyn, who was horrified by the work's darkness and lack of transcendence. There was a bizarre cameo during the premiere when Pavel Apostolov, Shostakovich's near-contemporary and one of his most virulent detractors in 1948, collapsed and died of a heart attack in the auditorium. Shostakovich did not feel so much rid of an old enemy as reminded once again of his own approaching death. The public première took place three months later in Leningrad with Vishnevskaya and the bass Mark Reshetin. Shostakovich had enjoyed a holiday and was in considerably better spirits.

His work of the next year oscillated between public and intensely private music. He contributed a set of choruses, *Loyalty*, Op 136, to mark Lenin's centenary, but also finished the film music for *King Lear*, Op 137. In autumn 1970, after yet another period in the clinic run by Gavriel Ilizarov, who pioneered the process of distraction osteogenesis and external framing of rebuilt bone, Shostakovich completed the String Quartet No 13 in B flat minor, Op 138, and the unpromising-sounding *March of the Soviet Police*, Op 139. He also began making sketches for what would be his last symphony.

The beginning of 1971 must have seemed to Russians like a disturbing return to the Stalinist past. Brezhnev and his hard-line followers attempted to impose a doctrine of unlimited sovereignty over the client states of Eastern Europe, and also over Communist Party members in the West and Asia. A dangerous conflict rumbled along the Sino-Soviet border. More acutely than at any time since 1962, the world seemed poised on the brink of catastrophe. More than at any time since the McCarthy witch-hunts of the late 1940s and early 1950s, "Communism" was a by-word for predatory ideological imperialism.

There was a smaller and stranger return of the past in Shostakovich's life as well, a first revival of *The Nose* in Russia since 1930. Shostakovich was disinclined to concede that the work had themes, somewhat contradicting his earlier insistence that the opera was a horror story rather than a joke, but its depiction of reified authority gone mad was as relevant in 1971 as it had been when first written. The long-lost score was actually found in the basement of the Bolshoi Theatre and despite the inevitable political shenanigans and despite Shostakovich's growing infirmity, he even attended some rehearsals, making the daring suggestion that a new passage (derived from Gogol) be interpolated by which one of the characters should leave the stage and recite the words "It's amazing that anyone should write about such a subject. We've never heard the like", while pointing accusingly at Shostakovich in the audience. The *yurodivy* was still alive, if not well.

Shostakovich returned to something close to this unexpected buffoonery in his penultimate work, the *Four Verses of Captain Lebyadkin*, Op 146, which he completed in January 1975. Coming so close to the end, this is a fascinating piece in which Lebyadkin is portrayed as a rascally "cockroach" deserving of our – rather than God's in Shostakovich's philosophical view – forgiveness precisely because of his rascality; Shostakovich would also have known that in the complex polyphonic theatre of Dostoevsky's *The Possessed* Marya Lebyadkin was a classic *yurodivaia*, whose spluttering wisdom is that of a holy fool.

Shostakovich had attempted a very different, and much grander self-association in another, somewhat earlier work, which might be accounted his last masterpiece. It is clear that in the *Suite on Verses by Michelangelo*, Op 145, there is

a complex identification with the great artist and poet. Benjamin Britten had been drawn to the subject in his *Seven Sonnets of Michelangelo,* written in 1940, and he and Shostakovich may well have discussed the work at Aldeburgh in the summer of 1972. Where Britten was drawn to the putative homoerotic strain in Michelangelo, Shostakovich was attracted by more sombre themes, such as "Truth", "Love", "Creation", "Night" and "Death", and by similarities with the Italian poet's near-contemporary William Shakespeare. There is an unmistakable echo of his *Hamlet*

At his favourite retreat, the dacha at Zhukovka, Shostakovich relaxes while Irina pays attention to a pet dog

music in the introduction to one of the movements, which are woven together with such formidable structural – one might almost say sculptural – control that "suite" hardly seems an adequate description for this late masterpiece. The Michelangelo settings, and particularly the finale, again make use of the *yurodivy* persona, but this time, somewhat as in the Blok cycle, *sub specie aeternitatis*; this is not the Fool mocking temporal authority, but Lear himself, frail and reduced, confronting the storm, as Shostakovich had confronted storms throughout his life. For a non-believer, it is a position of extraordinary bravery.

Shostakovich's own physical and moral courage were never clearer than in the final three years of his life. He no longer had Stalin, Zhdanov and Apostolov to torment him and with the intense loyalty and support of Irina and a small circle of friends no longer needed to fear the treachery of fair-weather friends and time-servers. In Maxim, who had settled on conducting as a profession, he had an interpreter who understood and could communicate the emotional deep structure of the work, albeit for a further fifteen years after his father's death under political constraints different only in degree and in rhetoric from those which had applied in 1936, 1948 and 1962.

However, the habits that develop in isolation and in permanent opposition become deeply engrained. The late Shostakovich resembles Galileo – who had appeared in Yevtushenko's text for the final movement of the Thirteenth Symphony – in his blend of obduracy and sheer survivalism. Like the great astronomer, Shostakovich was called upon to recant, but did so murmuring his equivalent of *Eppuor si muove*. What "moved" was what always stayed the same, the endless continuity-in-change of Russia and the Russian people.

Though seriously ill, Shostakovich had completed his final orchestral work, the Symphony No 15 in A, Op 141, in a concentrated burst of activity at Repino during July and August 1971. It is a deeply enigmatic work, on one view a simple farewell to the orchestra – almost every member of which is featured in solo – on another a grimly satirical work that triple-distils his disgust at Soviet society. The Brezhnev years saw a strange combination of stern centralised control and an apparent abandonment of discipline throughout society. Crime rose sharply, corruption poisoned the bureaucracy, while rates of alcoholism in the general population rose to terrifying levels. The mechanistic libertinism of the post-Revolutionary years seemed to have returned and Shostakovich captures it brilliantly in his opening movement, which is all awkward twos and threes cast in an almost cartoonish idiom. It begins with a thin chime which seems to shake the orchestra into activity. The implication is that the people now willingly dance to the official tune, or at least march drunkenly to it.

The second movement is starkly different, mournful night-music of the most profound kind, full of sadness but also sourly dissonant. There are efforts to make the presumed protagonist conform, over-bright chords which have little to do with the surrounding music, but they fail. There is, Shostakovich seems to be saying, an unbridgeable gulf between his sensibility and that of the surrounding culture. The same impression is confirmed in the third movement, which in some respects merely unpacks and then condenses the dramatic contrast of the opening two. The finale is as densely packed with quotations, misquotations and allusions as the rest of the symphony, and it has become a highly competitive musicological game to find them all. The most obvious is a reworking of the march from the Seventh Symphony, still recognisable but recast with what can only be disgust and resignation. The end is almost death-like, gasps and tremors, only just governed by a fibrillating heart.

Shostakovich suffered a further attack during the rehearsals, which were being conducted under his supervision by Maxim. If the Fifteenth was intended as a farewell to the orchestra that is how it stands. During his last three years, he concentrated on song-setting – including the magnificent Michelangelo suite and a sequence based on the poetry of Marina Tsvetayeva, his Op 143 – and writing what were to be his final string quartets. It is known that he had hoped to write an eventual twenty-four quartets, a complete cycle of the keys that had been the deep structure of his musical imagination for nearly sixty years. After hearing the final pages of the Fifteenth, it is almost impossible to imagine him writing another symphony, even if health had permitted.

As it was, he completed the Viola Sonata between periods in hospital, working at Repino as had been his habit. Shostakovich's health continue to worsen that summer as his cancer took hold. At the beginning of August he suffered a prolonged choking fit that seemed to damage the heart further. Shostakovich was returned to hospital where six days later he suffered respiratory failure. The agonic breathing must have sounded distressingly similar to those defeated gasps in the Fifteenth Symphony. At seven-thirty on the evening of August 9 1975, Dmitri Dmitriyevich Shostakovich died. On the same day and at approximately the same hour, thirty-three years earlier, Karl Elias had raised his baton in the sudden quiet of besieged Leningrad to begin the Seventh Symphony.

Shostakovich's civic funeral at Moscow Conservatoire was a bizarre affair. Orchestral musicians were on annual leave, so there was only recorded music in the Grand Hall. Many others who might have attended were at holiday dachas in Siberia or the Crimea. In his open coffin, Shostakovich himself looked as if he too had been lying in the sun, turned unnaturally pink by the mortician's make-up. It was his last disguise, and exactly the right colour. Ministry of Culture officials and KGB men scurried about anxiously to ensure that there would be no unseemly demonstrations, not of emotion, but of dissent. Then Tikhon Khrennikov rose to tell the assembled mourners what a good Communist Shostakovich had always been. Shostakovich's mortal remains were then taken to Novodevichi Cemetery where the coffin lid was sealed and the "good Communist", free of human gaze at last, was buried to the strains of the Soviet anthem.

Six weeks later, Fyodor Druzhinin gave the first performance of the Viola Sonata in Leningrad. Shostakovich's complex life was over. A complex afterlife was just about to begin.

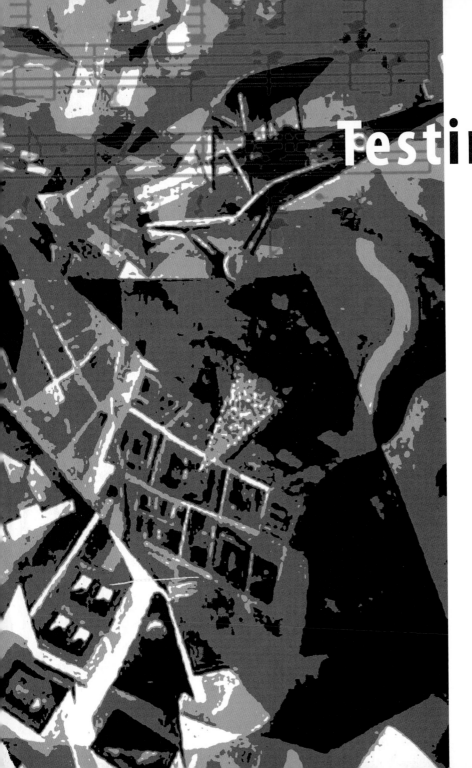

Testimony

Testimony

Sometime in the latter weeks of 1974, a young music journalist called Solomon Volkov brought a typescript to Shostakovich and had him sign each chapter. Immediately afterwards, Volkov applied for an exit visa to leave the Soviet Union for the United States. He sent ahead the pages that the composer had signed, lodging them first in a Swiss bank. Volkov was permitted to leave in 1976 and three years later, Harper & Row published *Testimony*, which purported to be the memoirs of Dmitri Dmitriyevich Shostakovich, tape-recorded and transcribed by Volkov.

There was an immediate outcry. Not until the putative "Hitler diaries" later in the decade was a text so closely examined and argued over. The Shostakovich presented in *Testimony* was a sour and vindictive renegade, viscerally hostile to the Soviet regime and scornful of fellow-artists as varied as Mayakovsky, Meyerhold, Mravinksy, and Prokofiev. The "good and loyal Communist" of the official obituaries was portrayed – or portrayed himself – as a fifth columnist who had concealed his true feelings for most of his adult life. In Russia, Volkov was vilified as a turncoat and a forger. His American publishers had scanned the pages closely for factual errors and, perhaps reassured by the composer's apparent approval, satisfied themselves that they were genuine. Even so, doubts persisted on both sides of the Iron Curtain. Those in the West who were prepared to accept that some of the book represented Shostakovich's words were inclined to believe that Volkov had embellished and enlarged the text substantially. On the left it was decried as a distortion, while both liberal and anti-Communist papers rushed to what seemed like a breach in the carefully defended Soviet consensus, which continued to demand absolute loyalty and orthodoxy from its artists.

There were immediate and genuine causes for concern. The composer's widow Irina at different times suggested that her husband had barely known Volkov, but also that she had demanded the return of the tape transcripts; two statements which do not entirely add up. However, somewhat later the matter seemed to be put beyond doubt when Maxim Shostakovich defected to the West and continued to insist that the work was not his father's but an act of politically motivated ventriloquism. Only much later did he reverse his position, stating on the BBC that *Testimony* did indeed represent his father's views. Galina also confirmed this.

An official photograph of Shostakovich at the piano taken in 1955

No aspect of Shostakovich studies is more tedious and more diversionary than the controversy surrounding the authenticity of Shostakovich's "memoir". There is even a whisper of latent anti-Semitism in the discussion of Volkov himself, who as a Jew was still more than usually vulnerable in 1970s Russia. Some motivations in the case are easily understood. Anti-Communist observers *wanted* to believe that *Testimony* was the work of a great artist who had been disgracefully treated by an evil regime. Communist and fellow-travelling observers *needed* to demonstrate that the book was a travesty. Tikhon Khrennikov, who had affirmed Shostakovich's political orthodoxy over his open coffin, most particularly wanted the book to be false because he was treated so harshly in it. More puzzling were the family's reactions. Irina told officials that at Shostakovich's behest she had asked Volkov to return the typescript. When told that it had already left the Soviet Union she threatened to block his exit visa. Puzzlingly, she only told this version on the eve of publication. Was she simply ensuring the authorities believed she had taken every possible step to prevent having the great Soviet composer – three times winner of the Order of Lenin and a Hero of Socialist Labour – lampooned by a forger. By the same token, was Maxim's continued insistence after his defection on the book's fraudulence simply a way of protecting family members left back in the Soviet Union?

There are few straight lines and absolute answers in the *Testimony* story. Volkov's own behaviour seems peculiar. Contrary to Irina's version, he claims to have had many meetings with Shostakovich at the composer's colony near Leningrad, and to have resumed the conversations when he moved to a Moscow apartment in the same building as Shostakovich. What of the claim in his preface to *Testimony* that he had tried to have the book published in the Soviet Union before Shostakovich's death? Clearly no state publisher would have touched it and its very existence would have put Volkov in considerable jeopardy. If this sequence of events was accurate, why had he sent the manuscript to Switzerland immediately it was signed? As so often in this tangled story, the question is self-answering: it was sent abroad precisely because it was dangerous, and the most likely means of publication at home would have been *samizdat*.

Volkov certainly knew Shostakovich. There is a photograph, printed in *Testimony* which shows him sitting with the composer and Irina. More significantly, the photograph is signed "To dear Solomon Moiseyevich Volkov with affection, D Shostakovich, 13.XI.74", an inscription which suggests a measure of intimacy between the two men. It also bears a subscription, apparently written as an afterthought: "A reminder of our conversations about Glazunov, Zoshchenko, Meyerhold. D.S.", which in turn suggests that any references to these figures in *Testimony* – and Glazunov in particular – can be accorded some veracity. However, one can now say with reasonable certainty that while *Testimony* almost certainly does accurately represent the real Shostakovich, at least in his later years, with some exceptions it equally certainly does not represent his actual words; that is, the book is true in spirit,

Beneath a bust of Lenin, Shostakovich addresses the All-Union Composers'
Congress in the Hall of Columns, House of Unions in Moscow, 1966

but still largely a forgery. The discovery in the text of substantial passages lifted verbatim from much earlier interviews proves that, in those cases at least, Volkov is something other than a loyal amanuensis.

What is important about *Testimony* is not so much what it said as what it sparked off. Its very existence is a catalyst for debate – Ian MacDonald's *The New Shostakovich* is in essence an extended revisionist attempt to find the author of *Testimony* in the works themselves – but like any true catalyst it remains unchanged by the processes it set off and remains what it always was, a highly convincing collage and an act of brilliant and insightful projection by a passionate music lover who had admired Shostakovich's work for many years. It is also important for the way it provoked open declaration of vested interest. When the leftist British critic Christopher Norris sneered at *Testimony* as an expression of Western hyper-subtlety and wishful belief that behind those slamming Socialist Realist climaxes there was a deeply conflicted and above all ironic artist who was simply putting on a show to save his life, he unconsciously revealed the left's own wishful thinking that behind those transparently ironic passages and sourly unconvincing apotheoses there was, after all, a loyal and committed Communist. One British Communist Party member told the present author with absolute confidence and a show of great sadness that *Testimony* was unquestionably real but that the opinions quoted were those of a very sick man, "out of his mind" with pain and medication. It is a clever rationalisation, particularly given Shostakovich's failing health in 1974, but it hardly squares with the clear-sighted and technically astute composer of the Michelangelo suite or the Viola Sonata.

Decades of criticism, disappointment, poor health and the loss of friends did doubtless colour Shostakovich's vision but there is no reason to think him changed in a fundamental way, as a moral agent, by his life's experiences. Consistency may be the hobgoblin of small minds, but it can also be the defining absolute of great ones. Shostakovich made clear and sharp distinctions between what men did and who they were, preferring the former – acts, public deeds, work – to any kind of psychological or ideological explanation. That is why he was able to admire Stravinsky the artist, while excoriating him as a thinker who had turned his back on country and traditions. The fact that sometimes such opinions squared with the "official" view does not mean that they were shaped by it, or pragmatically adjusted to fit it.

In his essence, something he would not himself have believed in other than as a sum of acts, Shostakovich was not a political animal but a moralist. He had a profound but non-ideological sense of social and ethical duty, and was genetically attached to a long Russian intellectual tradition that emphasised human improvement as a practical and philosophical absolute. Shostakovich also subscribed unquestioningly to the twin ideas of Russian exceptionalism – a conviction that Western ideas were alien to Russia's unique philosophical and cultural history – and of "Russia" as a unique and universal moral force. This was expressed in the untranslatable concept *Dusha* which means something close to "spirit" or "world-soul" and which enjoins a commitment to individual integrity, aesthetics and strong, practical moral awareness. All that did not serve those ends was anti-people. Shostakovich understood good but he equally understood evil, which is rarer, and which he would have seen in anything that did not contribute to that central *troika* of principled ends. Experience taught him that evil can not always be defeated by direct confrontation, but is always susceptible to the sole qualities it is incapable of detecting: humour and irony.

The Shostakovich of *Testimony* – who is inescapably Volkov's Shostakovich – is infinitely less interesting than the Shostakovich of the symphonies and the string quartets, the concertos, chamber music, song cycles and the magnificent *Lady Macbeth of Mtsensk*. He palpably believed that making music was a moral act and that in a godless world the artist brokered a relationship between power and people. Take away their programmatic titles, their texts, associations, criticisms and Decrees and his works almost invariably suggest that there are points of balance in a precarious world. He was a dialectician to the degree that he understood dissonance was the engine of progress, but Shostakovich fundamentally believed in harmony. His key signatures were beacons, points of light in the surrounding darkness.

That he was unable to escape history was not the tragedy in Shostakovich's life, but the source of his dark comedy. Russian to his very last breath, he understood that art is never "pure" and never entirely for itself, and yet all his life he aspired to an art that rose above politics, compromise, ideas and fashion and became the truest expression of the one other thing in which Shostakovich placed a lifetime's faith; probably it came down to him in the womb.

Even if we can believe only the sentiments, if not the actual text, of *Testimony*, Shostakovich's credo is to be found in these words about his re-orchestration of *Boris Godunov*:

(The people are the base of everything. The people are here and the rulers are there. The rule forced on the people is immoral and fundamentally anti-people. The best intentions of individuals don't count. That's Mussorgsky's position and I dare hope that it is also mine. I was also caught up in Mussorgsky's certainty that the contradictions between the rulers and the oppressed people were insoluble, which meant that the people had to suffer cruelly without end, and become ever more embittered. The government, in its attempt to establish itself, was decaying, putrefying. Chaos and state collapse lay ahead, as prophesied by the last two scenes of the opera. I expected it to happen in 1939...It was clear to everyone that war was coming, sooner or later it was coming. And I thought it would follow the plot of *Boris Godunov*... '*Dark darkness, impenetrable!*' And '*Sorrow, sorrow for Russia, weep, oh, weep Russian people! Hungry people*' cries the *Yurodivy*...)

130

Opus list

1916

Ode to Liberty (pf; does not survive)

1917

Funeral March for the Victims of the Revolution (pf; does not survive)

1918

The Gypsies (opera; destroyed 1926)
Rusalochka (ballet; destroyed 1926)

1919

Op. 1 Scherzo in F# minor (orchestra; f.p. Moscow, March 20 1925)

1920

Op. 2 Eight Preludes (pf)

1921

Op. 4 *Two Krylov Fables* (mez-sop, orchestra)
Rimsky-Korsakov, *I Waited For Thee in a Grotto* (orchestration)

1922

Op. 3 Theme and Variations in B flat (orchestra)
Op. 5 *Three Fantastic Dances* (orchestra)
Op. 6 Suite in F# (2 pf; in memoriam D.B. Shostakovich; f.p. Moscow, March 20 1925)

1923

(symphonic draft; interrupted by illness)
Op. 8 Piano Trio No 1 in C minor (f.p Moscow, March 20 1925)

1924

Op. 9 Three Pieces (vc, pf; lost)
Op. 7 Scherzo (pf, orchestra) (symphony resumed)
Op. 11a Prelude (string octet; in memoriam Volodya Kurchavov)

1925

Op. 10 Symphony No 1 in F minor (f.p. Leningrad, May 12 1926)
Op. 11b Scherzo (string octet)
(first publications: Scherzo in F# minor, First Symphony, Prelude)

1926

Op. 12 Piano Sonata No 1 (f.p. Moscow, January 9 1927) (destroys early works, inc. *Revolutionary Symphony*)

1927

Op. 13 *Aphorisms* (pf)
Op. 14 Symphony No 2 in B *To October* (f.p. Leningrad, November 5)
(First Symphony conducted in Berlin by Bruno Walter)

1928

Op. 15 *The Nose* (opera; suite f.p. Moscow, November 25; concert perf. Moscow, June 16 1929; staged Leningrad, January 23 1930)
Op. 16 *Tahiti Trot*
Op. 17 Two Scarlatti Pieces
(begins *Six Japanese Romances*)
(First Symphony conducted in New York by Leopold Stokowski)

1929

Op. 18 *New Babylon* (film music; suppressed; f.p. Paris, 1975)
Op. 19 *The Bedbug* Two pieces for *Columbus*
Op. 20 Symphony No 3 in E flat *First of May* (f.p. Leningrad, January 24 1930)
Op. 23 Two pieces for Erwin Dressel's opera *Armer Columbus* (orchestra)

Op. 24 *The Shot* (theatre music; lost)

1930

Op. 22 *The Golden Age* (ballet suite; f.p. Leningrad, October)

Op. 25 *Soil* (theatre music; lost)

1931

Op. 27 *The Bolt* (ballet suite; f.p. Leningrad, April 1931)

Op. 26 *Alone* (film music)

Op. 28 *Rule Britannia!*

Op. 30 *Golden Mountains* (film music)

Op. 31 *Allegedly Murdered* (revue)

1932

(Begins symphony, *From Karl Marx to Our Own Days*; abandoned)

Op. 21 *Six Japanese Romances* (f.p. Leningrad, April 24 1966)

Op. 32 *Hamlet* (theatre music; f.p. Moscow, May 19)

Op. 33 *Counterplan* (film music)

Op. 29 *Lady Macbeth of Mtsensk District* (opera; f.p. Leningrad/Moscow, January 1934)

1933

Op. 34 *Twenty-Four Preludes* (pf)

Op. 35 Piano Concerto No 1 in C minor

1934

Op. 37 *The Human Comedy* (theatre music)

Suite No 1 (dance band)

Op. 38 *Love and Hate* (film score)

Op. 40 Cello Sonata in D minor (f.p. Leningrad, December 25)

Op. 36 *Tale of a Priest and his Servant Balda* (comic opera)

Op. 41/1 *Maxim's Youth* (film music)

Op. 41/2 *Girlfriends* (film music)

1935

Op. 39 *The Limpid Stream* (ballet suite; f.p. Leningrad, June; Moscow, November)

Op. 42 *Five Fragments* (f.p. Leningrad, April 26 1965)

1936

Op. 43 Symphony No 4 in C minor (rehearsals stopped; f.p. Moscow, December 30 1961)

Op. 44 *Salute To Spain* (theatre music; play banned)

1937

Op. 45 *Maxim's Return* (film music)

Op. 46 *Four Pushkin Romances*

Op. 48 *Volochayesk Days* (film music)

Op. 47 Symphony No 5 in D minor (f.p. Leningrad, November 21; New York, March 1938)

(begins operetta *The Twelve Chairs*; abandoned)

(begins "Lenin Symphony"; abandoned)

Op. 49 String Quartet No 1 in C

Suite No 2 (dance band)

Op. 52 *Friends* (film music)

Op. 53 *The Man With A Gun* (film music)

Op. 50 *The Vyborg Side* (film music)

Op. 51 Music to the film *Friends*

Op. 51a Vocalise from *Friends* (chorus)

1939

Op. 55 *The Great Citizen* (film music)

Op. 56 *The Silly Little Mouse* (film music; lost or destroyed)

Op. 54 Symphony No 6 in B minor (f.p. Leningrad, November 5)

1940

Modest Mussorgsky, *Boris Godunov* (re-orchestration; f.p. November 4 1959)

Op. 57 Piano Quintet in G minor

Op. 58/2 *King Lear* (theatre music; f.p. March 1941)

Three Pieces (vn)

Op. 59 *The Adventures of Korzinkina* (film music)

(opera *Katyusha Maslova* begun and abandoned)

1941

Vow of the People's Commissar (choral)

The Fearless Regiments Are On The Move (choral)

(many songs and arrangements for military use)

Op. 60 Symphony No 7 in C *To The City of Leningrad* (f.p. Kuibyshev, March 5 1942; Moscow, March 29; Leningrad, August 9)

Дмитрий Дмитриевич Шостакович

1942

Op. 63 *Native Leningrad*
Solemn March (military band)
Op. 62 *Six Romances on Verses by English Poets*

1943

Op. 61 Piano Sonata No 2 in B minor
(with Aram Khachaturian) *Song of the Red Army*
Op. 65 Symphony No 8 in C minor (f.p. Moscow,
November 4)

1944

Op. 64 *Zoya* (film music)
Op. 67 Piano Trio No 2 in E minor (f.p. Moscow,
November 14)
Op. 68 String Quartet No 2 in A (f.p. Moscow,
November 14)
Op. 69 *Children's Notebook* (pf)
Op. 66 *Russian River* (spectacle)

1945

Op. 70 Symphony No 9 in E flat (f.p. Leningrad,
November 3)
Op. 71 *Simple Folk* (film music; released 1956)
Op. 72 *Victorious Spring* (incidental music)

1946

Op. 73 String Quartet no 3 in F (f.p. Mosco,
December 16)

1947

Op. 74 *Poem of the Motherland* (cantata)
Op. 76 *Pirogov* (film music)
Three Pieces for Orchestra (unpublished)

1948

Op. 77 Violin Concerto No 1 in A minor (f.p.
Leningrad, October 29 1955)
Portrait Gallery (Rayok) (cantata)
Op. 75 *The Young Guard* (film music)
Op. 78 *Michurin* (film music)
Op. 79 *From Jewish Folk Poetry* (f.p. Moscow,
January 15 1955;
orchestrated 1963)
Op. 80 *Meeting on the Elbe* (film music)

1949

Op. 81 *Song of the Forests* (oratorio)
Op. 82 *The Fall of Berlin* (film music)
Op. 83 String Quartet No 4 in D (f.p. Moscow,
December 3 1953)

1950

Op. 84 *Two Lermontov Songs*
Op. 85 *Belinsky* (film music; first screened June 4
1953)

1951

Op. 87 *Twenty Four Preludes and Fugues* (pf;
f.p.Leningrad,
December 23-28)
Op. 86 *Four Dolmatovsky Songs*
Op. 88 *Ten Poems on Revolutionary Texts* (chorus;
f.p. Moscow,
October 10)
Op. 89 *The Unforgettable Year 1919* (film music)

1952

Op. 90 *The Sun Shines Over Our Motherland*
(cantata)
Op. 91 *Four Pushkin Monologues*
Op. 92 String Quartet No 5 in B flat (f.p. Moscow,
November 13)
Seven Dances of the Dolls

1953

Op. 93 Symphony No 10 in E minor (f.p.
December 17)
Op. 94 Concertino for Two Pianos (f.p. Moscow,
January 20 1954)
Hamlet (theatre music)
Op. 95 *Seven Ribers*
Op. 96 *Festival Overture*

1955

Op. 97 *The Gadfly* (film music)
Op. 98 *Five Dolmatovsky Songs (Songs of Our
Days)*

1956

Op. 99 *The First Echelon* (film music)

Op. 100 *Six Spanish Songs*
Op. 101 String Quartet No 6 in G

1957

Op. 102 Piano Concerto No 2 in F
Op. 103 Symphony No 11 in G minor *The Year 1905* (f.p Moscow, October 30)
Op. 104 *Two Russian Folk Songs (Cultivation)*

1958

Op. 105 *Moscow, Cheryomuschki* (operetta; f.p. Moscow, January 24)
Op. 106 Modest Mussorgsky, *Khovanschina* (re-orchestration; f.p. Moscow, May 23 1959)

1960

Op. 107 Cello Concerto No 1 in E flat (f.p. Leningrad, October 4)
Op. 108 String Quartet No 7 in F # minor (f.p. Leningrad, May 15)
Op. 109 *Five Satires (Pictures of the Past)* (f.p. Leningrad, February 22 1961)
Op. 110 String Quartet No 8 in C minor (f.p.Leningrad, October 2)
Op. 111 *Five Days, Five Nights* (film music)
Op. 112 Symphony No 12 in D minor *The Year 1917* (f.p. Moscow, October 1)
Novorossiisk Chimes

1962

Modest Mussorgsky, *Songs and Dances of Death* (orchestration)
Op. 124 *Two Davidenko Choruses* (arranged)
Op. 113 Symphony No 13 in B flat minor *Babi Yar* (f.p. December 18)
Op. 114 *Katerina Ismailova* (revision of *Lady Macbeth of Mtsensk*; f.p. Leningrad, December 26; Moscow, January 8 1963)
Op. 114a Suite of five fragments from *Katerina Ismailova*
Op. 114b Music to the film *Katerina Ismailova*
Op. 114c Passacaglia from *Katerina Ismailova*

1963

Op. 125 Robert Schumann, Cello Concerto (re-orchestration)
Op. 115 *Overture on Russian and Khirgiz Thmes*
Prelude and Fugue No 15 (arranged for 2 pf)
Tarantella from *The Gadfly* (arranged for 2pf)

1964

Op. 116 *Hamlet* (theatre music)
(Announces work on opera *The Quiet Don*; abandoned 1967, (probably with little real work done)
Op. 117 String Quartet No 9 in E flat (f.p. Moscow, November 20)
Op. 118 String Quartet No 10 in A flat (f.p. Moscow, November 20)
Op. 119 *The Execution of Stepan Razin* (cantata; f.p. Moscow, December 28)

1965

Op. 120 *A Year As Long as a Lifetime* (film music)
Op. 121 *Five Romances on Texts from Krokodil* (f.p. Leningrad, May 28 1966)
(Film version of *Katerina Ismailova*; first screened September 25 1966)

1966

Op. 122 String Quartet No 11 in F minor (f.p. Moscow, March 25)
Op. 123 *Preface to My Collected Works and Brief Reflections on This Preface*
Op. 126 Cello Concerto No 2 in G (f.p. September 25 1966)

1967

Op. 127 *Seven Romances of Poems of Alexander Blok*
Op. 128 *Spring, spring* (song)
Op. 129 Violin Concerto No 2 in C # minor (f.p. Bolshevo, September 13)
Op. 130 *Funeral-Triumphal Prelude*
Op. 131 *October* (symphonic poem)
Op. 132 *Sofia Perovskaya* (film music)

1968

Fleishman, *Rothschild's Violin* (orchestration; f.p. Leningrad, March)

Op. 133 String Quartet No 12 in D flat (f.p. Moscow, June 14)

Op. 134 Violin Sonata (f.p. Moscow, January 8)

1969

Boris Tishchenko, Cello Concerto No 1 (re-orchestration)

Op. 135 Symphony No 14 (f.p. Leningrad, September 29)

1970

Op. 136 *Loyalty* (eight choruses for Lenin's birthday)

Op. 137 *King Lear* (film music)

Op. 138 String Quartet No 13 in B flat minor (f.p. Moscow, December 11)

Op. 139 *March of the Soviet Police*

1971

Op. 140 *Six Romances on Verses by English Poets* (orchestration)

Op. 141 Symphony No 15 in A (f.p. Moscow, January 8 1972)

1973

Op. 142 String Quartet No 14 in F# (f.p. Moscow, October 30)

Op. 143 *Six Romances on Poems by Marina Tsvetayeva* (f.p.Moscow, December 27)

1974

Op. 143a *Six Tsvetatyeva Songs* (ochestration)

Op. 144 String Quartet No 15 in E flat minor (f.p. Leningrad, October 25)

Op. 145 *Suite on Verses by Michelangelo* (f.p.Leningrad, December 23)

1975

Op. 145a *Michelangelo Suite* (orchestration)

Beethoven, *Song of the Flea* (orchestration)

Op. 146 *Four Verses of Captain Lebyadkin*

Op. 147 Viola Sonata (f.p. posth. Leningrad, October 1)

Index of Names

A

Abraham, Gerald. 34
Akhmatova, Anna. 63, 76, 115
Akimov, Nikolai. 42
Alexander II. 45
Alexandrov, Alexander. 37
Apostolov, Pavel. 117
Asafiev, Boris. 48

B

Ballantine, Christopher. 54
Bartók, Béla. 21
Beethoven, Ludwig. 56, 71
Berg, Alban. 36
Beria, Lavrenti. 59
Bezymensky, Alexander. 34
Borisovsky, Vadim. 117
Bowen, Meiron. 34
Brezhnev, Leonid. 108, 114,
Britten, Benjamin. 113, 119
Bukharin, Nikolai. 36
Burns, Robert. 17
Bussoni, Ferrucio. 19

C

Cardus, Neville. 17
Carter, Elliot. 114
Catherine the Great. 32
Chernyshevsky, Nikolai. 10, 32
Churchill, Winston. 68, 75
Copland, Aaron. 5
Costello, Elvis. 7
Craft, Robert. 8, 10

D

Davidenko, Alexander. 47
Demchenko, Maria. 53

Dolmatovsky, Yevgeny. 84
Druzhinin, Fyodor. 112, 117, 121
Dzerzhinsky, Ivan. 49

E

Eisenstein, Sergei. 76
Eliasberg, Karl. 66
Eliot, T.S. 44

F

Fadayev, A.A. 2

G

Glazunov, Alexander. 15, 18, 19,
23
Gliasser, Ignati. 17, 18
Glikman, Isaak. 40, 49, 96, 99,
100
Glivenko, Tanya. 20
Gogol, Nikolai. 35, 85, 118
Gorky, Maxim. 42, 49
Gozzi, Carlo. 36

H

Haitink, Bernard. 68
Haydn, Joseph. 48
Hitler, Adolf. 29, 62

I

Ilizarov, Gavriel. 118

J

Janáček, Leoš 21

K

Kainova, Margarita. (Second
wife). 91, 92
Kennedy, John, Fitzgerald. 10
Khachaturian, Aram. 65, 77
Khrushchev, Nikita. 6, 77, 92
Kirov, Sergei. 47
Kirsanov, Semyon. 34
Klemperer, Otto. 53
Kokaoulina, Sofia Vasilievna
(Mother). 16
Kondrashin, Kyrill. 57, 104
Kozintsev, Grigori. 92, 109, 114
Krennikov, Tikhon. 77. 78
Kuba, Natasha. 21
Kuibyshev, Valerian. 63, 65, 68
Kurchavov, Volodya. 22
Kustodiev, Boris. 20

L

Lenin, Vladimir Ilich. 18, 33, 101
Lebedinsky, Lev. 96
Leskov, Nikolai. 44
List, Kurt. 29
Liszt, Franz. 21
Litvinova, Flora. 104
Litvinov, Mikhail. 104
Litvinov, Maxim. 59
Lunacharsky, Anatoli. 19, 32,

M

MacDairmid, Hugh. 2, 9
Macdonald, Ian. 34, 54, 68, 69,
70
Mahler, Gustav. 56
Mailer, Norman. 2, 4
Malenkov, Georgi. 90
Malko, Nikolai. 23

Picture credits

The author and publisher wish
to express their thanks to the
following sources of illustrative
material . RIA Novosti, Getty
Images, Corbis.